D1175020

ANALYZING THE ISSUES

CRITICAL PERSPECTIVES ON EFFECTIVE POLICING AND POLICE BRUTALITY

Edited by Cyndy Aleo

Enslow Publishing

101 W. 23rd Street

Published in 2018 by Enslow Publishing, LLC
101 W. 23rd Street, Suite 240, New York, NY 10011

Copyright © 2018 by Enslow Publishing, LLC

Library of Congress Cataloging-in-Publication Data

Names: Aleo, Cyndy, editor.
Title: Critical perspectives on effective policing and police brutality / edited by Cyndy Aleo.
Description: New York : Enslow Publishing, [2018] | Series: Analyzing the issues | Audience: Grades 7-12. | Includes bibliographical references and index.
Identifiers: LCCN 2017018161 | ISBN 9780766091702 (library bound) | ISBN 9780766095588 (paperback)
Subjects: LCSH: Police—United States—Juvenile literature. | Law enforcement—United States—Juvenile literature. | Police brutality—United States—Juvenile literature.
Classification: LCC HV8139 .C77 2017 | DDC 363.2/30973—dc23
LC record available at https://lccn.loc.gov/2017018161

Printed in China

To Our Readers: We have done our best to make sure all website addresses in this book were active and appropriate when we went to press. However, the author and the publisher have no control over and assume no liability for the material available on those websites or on any websites they may link to. Any comments or suggestions can be sent by email to customerservice@enslow.com.

Excerpts and articles have been reproduced with the permission of the copyright holders.

Photo Credits: Cover Robert Nickelsberg/Getty Images; cover and interior pages graphic elements Thaiview/Shutterstock.com (cover top, pp. 1, 4-5), gbreezy/Shutterstock.com (magnifying glass), Ghornstern/Shutterstock.com (additional interior pages).

CONTENTS

INTRODUCTION 4

CHAPTER 1
WHAT ACADEMICS, EXPERTS, AND
RESEARCHERS SAY 6

CHAPTER 2
WHAT THE GOVERNMENT AND
POLITICIANS SAY 76

CHAPTER 3
WHAT THE COURTS SAY 99

CHAPTER 4
WHAT ADVOCACY
ORGANIZATIONS SAY 137

CHAPTER 5
WHAT THE MEDIA SAY 182

CHAPTER 6
WHAT ORDINARY PEOPLE SAY.............. 195

CONCLUSION 212

BIBLIOGRAPHY..................................... 214
CHAPTER NOTES.................................... 216
GLOSSARY 226
FOR MORE INFORMATION..................... 227
INDEX 228
ABOUT THE EDITOR.............................. 231

INTRODUCTION

From the beating of Rodney King in 1991 to the swell of protests that began with the death of Trayvon Martin and galvanized after the death of Michael Brown in Ferguson, Missouri, more attention is being paid to the actions of police officers and how their procedures affect those they are charged with serving and protecting. In the past several years, the United States has seen a rise in tensions between police forces and citizens, with protests over police use of force and calls to action demanding more police accountability occurring on a regular basis.

The prevalence of the internet has led to increased scrutiny of police actions, with videos of alleged use of inappropriate force appearing on social media and calls for action bubbling right behind them. Meanwhile, some believe that police actions are justified, that the Black Lives Matter movement is a hate group, and respond with social media hashtags like #BlueLivesMatter.

In many cases, these incidents are tried by the public based on evidence seen through the view of the internet. However, police unions—and many politicians—disagree with the public's perception as well as requests to change procedures, including the use of body cameras.

We'll take a look at both sides of the issue in the chapters that follow, including research, court rulings, and opinions from average citizens on both sides of the issue, examining what police brutality actually is, as well as the challenges police forces face in the current cultural climate. Hopefully, by the end of this book, you will be able to form your own opinion about how the police are interacting with the public they serve and protect, and have a new perspective with which to examine current events that involve police actions.

CHAPTER 1

WHAT ACADEMICS, EXPERTS, AND RESEARCHERS SAY

Researchers are always looking for safer and more efficient ways to police. From studying how to best address "hot spots," or areas of high crime incidences, to addressing how police interact with the communities they serve by altering the racial and ethnic makeup of police forces, efforts are underway to address both the issues facing current police and the criticisms advocates have in how police forces function.

This chapter looks at some of the research that has been conducted. Examining available data on racial disparities in use of force by police may be the best place to begin, as John Wihbey and Leighton Walter Kille's "Excessive or Reasonable Force by Police? Research on Law Enforcement and Racial Conflict" does. Kille also looks at research on areas where crime seems to concentrate, known as hot spots, in "Hot Spots Policing and Crime Prevention Strategies: Ongoing Research." Of course, once those hot spots have been identified, there are several ways proposed to combat crime as examined by James P. McElvain, Augustine J. Kposowa, and Brian C. Gray in "Testing a Crime Control Model: Does Strategic and Directed Deployment of Police Officers Lead to Lower Crime?" There may be a challenge in making changes to current police procedures as determined by the management style within each police force, as noted in "Transactional and Transformational Leadership" by Steve McCartney and Rick Parent. And finally, a UK study takes a look at how mandating racial and ethnic diversity to mirror the communities police serve may impact how the police operate internally as well as their interactions with the public in Bela Bhugowandeen's "Diversity in the British Police: Adapting to a Multicultural Society."

Of course, no research is perfect, and each study notes that any research into police actions is rife with codicils: Reporting of data is often incomplete and subject to bias. Hot spots, for example, may be the result of a concentration of criminals, but also due to economic status. And if particular racial groups share an economic status and therefore a neighborhood that becomes a hot spot, will that group be represented in a disproportionate number of interactions with police?

"EXCESSIVE OR REASONABLE FORCE BY POLICE? RESEARCH ON LAW ENFORCEMENT AND RACIAL CONFLICT," BY JOHN WIHBEY AND LEIGHTON WALTER KILLE, FROM *JOURNALIST'S RESOURCE*, JULY 28, 2016

Allegations of the use of excessive force by U.S. police departments continue to generate headlines more than two decades after the 1992 Los Angeles riots brought the issue to mass public attention and spurred some law enforcement reforms. Recent deaths at the hands of police have fueled a lively debate across the nation in recent years.

In a number of closely watched cases involving the deaths of young black men, police have been acquitted, generating uproar and concerns about equal justice for all. On Staten Island, N.Y., the July 2014 death of Eric Garner because of the apparent use of a "choke-hold" by an officer sparked outrage. A month later in Ferguson, Mo., the fatal shooting of teenager Michael Brown by officer Darren Wilson ignited protests, and a grand jury's decision not to indict Wilson triggered further unrest. In November, Tamir Rice was shot by police in Cleveland, Ohio. He was 12 years old and playing with a toy pistol. On April 4, 2015, Walter L. Scott was shot by a police officer after a routine traffic stop in North Charleston, S.C. The same month, Freddie Gray died while in police custody in Baltimore, setting off widespread unrest. The policeman in the South Carolina case, Michael T. Slager, was charged with murder based on a cellphone video. In Baltimore, the driver of the police van in which Gray died, Caesar Goodson, was charged with second-degree murder, with lesser charges for five other officers. There have been no indictments in the earlier cases.

These follow other recent incidents and controversies, including an April 2014 finding by the U.S. Department of Justice (DOJ), following a two-year investigation, that the Albuquerque, N.M., police department "engages in a pattern or practice of use of excessive force, including deadly force, in violation of the Fourth Amendment," and a similar DOJ finding in December 2014 with regard to the Cleveland police department. In March 2015, the DOJ also issued a report detailing a pattern of "clear racial disparities" and "discriminatory intent" on the part of the Ferguson, Mo., police department.

As the *Washington Post* reported in July 2015, a pervasive problem that is only now beginning to be recognized is the lack of training for officers dealing with mentally ill persons, a situation that can often escalate to violent confrontations.

The events of 2014-2016 have prompted further calls by some police officials, politicians and scholars for another round of national reforms, in order to better orient "police culture" toward democratic ideals.

TWO SIDES, DISPARATE VIEWS

Surveys in recent years with minority groups — Latinos and African-Americans, in particular — suggest that confidence in law enforcement is relatively low, and large portions of these communities believe police are likely to use excessive force on suspects. A 2014 Pew Research Center survey confirms stark racial divisions in response to the Ferguson police shooting, as well, while Gallup provides insights on historical patterns of distrust. According to a Pew/*USA Today* poll conducted in August 2014, Americans of all races collectively "give relatively low marks to police departments around the country for holding officers accountable for misconduct, using the appropriate amount of force, and treating racial and ethnic groups equally." Social scientists who have done extensive field research and interviews note the deep sense of mistrust embedded in many communities.

Numerous efforts have been made by members of the law enforcement community to ameliorate these situations, including promising strategies such as "community policing." Still, from a police perspective, law enforcement in the United States continues to be dangerous work — America has a relatively higher homicide rate compared to other developed nations, and has many more guns per capita. Citizens seldom learn of the countless incidents where officers choose to hold fire and display restraint under extreme stress. Some research has shown that even well-trained officers are not consistently able to fire their weapon in time before a suspect holding a gun can raise it and fire first; this makes split-second judgments, even under "ideal" circumstances, exceptionally difficult. But as the FBI points out, police departments and officers sometimes do not handle the aftermath of incidents well in terms of transparency and clarity, even when force was reasonably applied, fueling public confusion and anger.

In 2013, 49,851 officers were assaulted in the line of duty, with an injury rate of 29.2 percent, according to the FBI. Twenty-seven were murdered that year.

FBI DIRECTOR: NO "RELIABLE GRASP" OF PROBLEM

How common are such incidents of police use of force, both lethal and non-lethal, in the United States? Has there been progress in America? The indisputable reality is that we do not fully know. FBI Director James B. Comey stated the following in a remarkable February 2015 speech:

> Not long after riots broke out in Ferguson late last summer, I asked my staff to tell me how many people shot by police were African-American in this country. I wanted to see trends. I wanted to see information. They couldn't give it to me, and it wasn't their fault. Demographic data regarding officer-involved shootings is not consistently reported to us through our Uniform Crime Reporting Program. Because reporting is voluntary, our data is incomplete and therefore, in the aggregate, unreliable.

> I recently listened to a thoughtful big city police chief express his frustration with that lack of reliable data. He said he didn't know whether the Ferguson police shot one person a week, one a year, or one a century, and that in the absence of good data, "all we get are ideological thunderbolts, when what we need are ideological agnostics who use information to try to solve problems." He's right.

> The first step to understanding what is really going on in our communities and in our country is to gather more and better data related to those we arrest, those we confront for breaking the law and jeopardizing public safety, and those who confront

us. "Data" seems a dry and boring word but, without it, we cannot understand our world and make it better.

How can we address concerns about "use of force," how can we address concerns about officer-involved shootings if we do not have a reliable grasp on the demographics and circumstances of those incidents? We simply must improve the way we collect and analyze data to see the true nature of what's happening in all of our communities.

The FBI tracks and publishes the number of "justifiable homicides" reported by police departments. But, again, reporting by police departments is voluntary and not all departments participate. That means we cannot fully track the number of incidents in which force is used by police, or against police, including non-fatal encounters, which are not reported at all.

Without a doubt, training for police has become more standardized and professionalized in recent decades. A 2008 paper in the *Northwestern University Law Review* provides useful background on the evolving legal and policy history relating to the use of force by police and the "reasonableness" standard by which officers are judged. Related jurisprudence is still being defined, most recently in the 2007 *Scott v. Harris* decision by the U.S. Supreme Court. But inadequate data and reporting — and the challenge of uniformly defining excessive versus justified force — make objective understanding of trends difficult.

A 2015 report conducted for the Justice Department analyzed 394 incidents involving deadly police force in Philadelphia from 2007-2014. It found that "officers do not receive regular, consistent training on the department's deadly force policy"; that early training among recruits is sometimes inadequate in regard to these issues; that investigations into such incidents are not consistent; and that officers "need more less-lethal options."

For perhaps the best overall summary of police use-of-force issues, see "A Multi-method Evaluation of Police Use of Force Outcomes: Final Report to the National Institute of Justice," a 2010 study conducted by some of the nation's leading criminal justice scholars.

AVAILABLE STATISTICS, BACKGROUND ON USE OF FORCE

The Justice Department releases statistics on this and related issues, although these datasets are only periodically updated: It found that in 2008, among people who had contact with police, "an estimated 1.4% had force used or threatened against them during their most recent contact, which was not statistically different from the percentages in 2002 (1.5%) and 2005 (1.6%)." In terms of the volume of citizen complaints, the Justice Department also found that there were 26,556 complaints lodged in 2002; this translates to "33 complaints per agency and 6.6 complaints per 100 full-time sworn officers." However, "overall rates were higher among large municipal police departments, with 45 complaints per agency, and 9.5 complaints per 100 full-time sworn officers." In 2011, about 62.9 million people had contact with the police.

In terms of the use of lethal force, aggregate statistics on incidents of all types are difficult to obtain from official sources. Some journalists are trying to rectify this; and some data journalists question what few official national statistics are available. The Sunlight Foundation explains some of the data problems, while also highlighting databases maintained by the Centers for Disease Control (CDC). The available data, which does not paint a complete national picture, nevertheless raise serious questions, Sunlight notes:

> [A]ccording to the CDC, in Oklahoma the rate at which black people are killed per capita by law enforcement is greater than anywhere else in the country. That statistic is taken from data collected for the years 1999-2011. During that same time period, Oklahoma's rate for all people killed by law enforcement, including all races, is second only to New Mexico. However, Oklahoma, the District of Columbia, Nevada and Oregon are all tied for the rate at which people are killed. (The CDC treats the District of Columbia as a state when collecting and displaying statistics.) In Missouri, where Mike Brown lived and died, black people are killed by law enforcement twice as frequently as white people. Nationwide, the rate at which black people are killed by law enforcement is 3 times higher than that of white people.

As mentioned, the FBI does publish statistics on "justifiable homicide" by law enforcement officers: The data show that there have been about 400 such incidents nationwide each year. However, FiveThirtyEight, among other journalism outlets, has examined the potential problems with these figures. News investigations suggest that the rates of deadly force usage are far from uniform. For example, Los Angeles saw an increase in such incidents in 2011, while Massachusetts saw more officers firing their weapon over the period 2009-2013.

The academic community has also provided some insights in this area. A 2008 study from Matthew J. Hickman of Seattle University, Alex R. Piquero of the University of Maryland and Joel H. Garner of the Joint Centers for Justice Studies reviewed some of the best studies and data sources available to come up with a more precise national estimate for incidents of non-lethal force. They note that among 36 different studies published since the 1980s, the rates of force asserted vary wildly, from a high of more than 30% to rates in the low single digits. The researchers analyze Police-Public Contact Survey (PPCS) data and Bureau of Justice Statistics Survey of Inmates in Local Jails (SILJ) data and conclude that an estimated 1.7% of all contacts result in police threats or use of force, while 20% of arrests do.

A 2012 study in the *Criminal Justice Policy Review* analyzed the patterns of behavior of one large police department — more than 1,000 officers — and found that a "small proportion of officers are responsible for a large proportion of force incidents, and that officers who frequently use force differ in important and significant ways from officers who use force less often (or not at all)." A 2007 study in *Criminal Justice and Behavior*, "Police Education, Experience and the Use of Force," found that officers with more experience and education may be less likely to use force, while a review of case studies suggests that specific training programs and accountability structures can lower the use of violence by police departments.

A 2016 working paper from the National Bureau of Economic Research (NBER) came to a conclusion that surprised some observers. Across the U.S., though blacks are 21.3 percent more likely to be involved in an altercation with police where a weapon is drawn, the researchers found no racial differences in police shootings: "Partitioning the data in myriad ways, we find no evidence of racial discrimination in officer-involved shootings. Investigating the intensive margin – the timing of shootings or how many bullets were discharged in the endeavor – there are no detectable racial differences."

Researchers continue to refine analytical procedures in order to make more accurate estimates based on police reports and other data.

CHARACTERISTICS OF SUSPECTS

A widely publicized report in October 2014 by ProPublica, a leading investigative and data journalism outlet, concluded that young black males are 21 times more likely to be shot by police than their white counterparts: "The 1,217 deadly police shootings from 2010 to 2012 captured in the federal data show that blacks, age 15 to 19, were killed at a rate of 31.17 per million, while just 1.47 per million white males in that age range died at the hands of police."

Research has definitively established that "racial profiling" by law enforcement exists — that persons of color are more likely to be stopped by police. FBI Director James Comey's 2015 comments are again relevant here:

[P]olice officers on patrol in our nation's cities often work in environments where a hugely disproportionate percentage of street crime is committed by young men of color. Something happens to people of good will working in that environment. After years of police work, officers often can't help but be influenced by the cynicism they feel.

A mental shortcut becomes almost irresistible and maybe even rational by some lights. The two young black men on one side of the street look like so many others the officer has locked up. Two white men on the other side of the street—even in the same clothes—do not. The officer does not make the same association about the two white guys, whether that officer is white or black. And that drives different behavior. The officer turns toward one side of the street and not the other. We need to come to grips with the fact that this behavior complicates the relationship between police and the communities they serve.

While the cases of Rodney King in 1991 and Amadou Diallo in 1999 heightened the country's awareness of race and policing, research has not uniformly corroborated the contention that minorities are more likely, on average, to be subject to acts of police force than are whites. A 2010 paper published in the *Southwestern Journal of Criminal Justice* reviewed more than a decade's worth of peer-reviewed studies and found that while many studies established a correlation between minority status and police use of force, many other studies did not — and some showed mixed results.

Of note in this research literature is a 2003 paper, "Neighborhood Context and Police Use of Force," that suggests police are more likely to employ force in higher-crime neighborhoods generally, complicating any easy interpretation of race as the decisive factor in explaining police forcefulness. The researchers, William Terrill of

Northeastern University and Michael D. Reisig of Michigan State University, found that "officers are significantly more likely to use higher levels of force when encountering criminal suspects in high crime areas and neighborhoods with high levels of concentrated disadvantage independent of suspect behavior and other statistical controls." Terrill and Reisig explore several hypothetical explanations and ultimately conclude:

> Embedded within each of these potential explanations is the influence of key sociodemographic variables such as race, class, gender, and age. As the results show, when these factors are considered at the encounter level, they are significant. However, the race (i.e., minority) effect is mediated by neighborhood context. Perhaps officers do not simply label minority suspects according to what Skolnick (1994) termed "symbolic assailants," as much as they label distressed socioeconomic neighborhoods as potential sources of conflict.

In studying the Seattle and Miami police departments, the authors of the 2010 National Institute of Justice report also conclude that "non-white suspects were less likely to be injured than white suspects ... where suspect race was available as a variable for analysis. Although we cannot speculate as to the cause of this finding, or whether it is merely spurious, it is encouraging that minority suspects were not *more likely* to be injured than whites."

USE OF TASERS AND OTHER "LESS LETHAL" WEAPONS

A 2011 report from the National Institute of Justice, "Police Use of Force, Tasers and Other Less-Lethal Weapons," examines the effectiveness and health outcomes of incidents involving CEDs (conducted energy devices), the most common of which is the Taser. The report finds that: (1) Injury rates vary widely when officers use force in general, ranging from 17% to 64% for citizens and 10% to 20% for officers; (2) Use of Tasers and other CEDs can reduce the statistical rate of injury to suspects and officers who might otherwise be involved in more direct, physical conflict — an analysis of 12 agencies and more than 24,000 use-of-force cases "showed the odds of suspect injury decreased by almost 60% when a CED was used"; and (3) A review of fatal Taser incidents found that many involved multiple uses of the device against the suspect in question.

A 2011 study, "Changes in Officer Use of Force Over Time: A Descriptive Analysis of a National Survey," documents trends in the use of non-lethal force by law enforcement officers (LEAs). The results indicate that CED use has risen significantly (to about 70% of LEAs), while baton use is down to 25% in 2008. "CED use was ranked among the most-used tactics from 2005 to 2008," the scholars conclude. "Excessive-force complaints against LEAs, internally generated, have more than doubled from 2003 to 2008. Officer injuries varied little from 2003 to 2008, but they are still only about half as common as suspect injuries. Also, only 20% of LEAs collect injury data in a database, complicating future research."

POTENTIAL IMPACT OF BODY CAMERAS

Video recordings of interactions between the police and the public have increased significantly in recent years as technology has improved and the number of distribution channels has expanded. Any standard

smartphone can now make a video — as was the case in the
Walter L. Scott shooting — and dash-mounted cameras in
police cars have become increasingly common.

The mandatory adoption of body cameras by police
has been suggested to increase transparency in interactions between law-enforcement officials and the public.
A 2014 study from the U.S. Department of Justice, "Police
Officer Body-Worn Cameras: Assessing the Evidence,"
reviews available research on the costs and benefits of
body-worn camera technology. The author, Michael D.
White of Arizona State University, identified five empirical
studies on body cameras, and assesses their conclusions.
In particular, a year after the Rialto, Calif., police department began requiring all officers to wear body cameras,
use of force by officers fell by 60% and citizen complaints
dropped by nearly 90%. The searcher notes:

> The decline in complaints and use of force may be
> tied to improved citizen behavior, improved police
> officer behavior, or a combination of the two. It
> may also be due to changes in citizen complaint
> reporting patterns (rather than a civilizing effect),
> as there is evidence that citizens are less likely to
> file frivolous complaints against officers wearing
> cameras. Available research cannot disentangle
> these effects; thus, more research is needed.

The studies also noted concerns about the cost of
the required devices, training and systems for storing video
footage; potential health and safety effects; and especially privacy concerns, both for citizens and the police.
In April 2015, a bill being considered in the Michigan State
legislature would exempt some body-camera footage
from the state's Freedom of Information (FOI) laws. Those

who spoke in favor of the law included a conservative Republican legislator and an ACLU representative.

PUBLIC OPINION AND MEDIA

The coverage of such incidents by mass media has been studied by researchers, some of whom have concluded that the press has often distorted and helped justify questionable uses of force. Finally, survey data continue to confirm the existence of undercurrents of racism and bias in America, despite demonstrable social progress; a 2014 Stanford study shows how awareness of higher levels of black incarceration can prompt greater support among whites for tougher policing and prison programs.

1. The article's authors cite research that suggests race has less to do with a disparity in reported police use of force incidents than the neighborhoods they take place in. Assuming this is correct, what could be done to reduce the number of incidents involving people of color?

2. Media coverage of incidents has been widespread, including through resharing on social media. Do you think a disproportionate amount of attention is paid to these incidents compared to the statistics? Why or why not?

"HOT SPOTS POLICING AND CRIME PREVENTION STRATEGIES: ONGOING RESEARCH," BY LEIGHTON WALTER KILLE, FROM *JOURNALIST'S RESOURCE*, JULY 11, 2013

Some areas have higher crime rates, and even within troubled neighborhoods, specific locations often stand out. Police have spent decades trying to perfect techniques for distributing resources efficiently to cope with these "hot spots." Increased patrols can produce significant reduction in crime in specific areas, but does criminal activity simply move elsewhere? While there have been anecdotal successes in some cities, is there a more-effective policing model that all law enforcement could adopt?

Research in this area continues to unfold as law enforcement officials pilot new techniques, and scholars isolate certain variables and try to reduce uncertainties. Many studies have been inconclusive or suggest that apparent police successes may be unique to a given circumstance.

For example, a 2005 Harvard University metastudy published in the *Journal of Experimental Criminology*, "Hot Spots Policing and Crime Prevention: A Systematic Review of Randomized Controlled Trials," examined the effects of five randomized controlled trials of concentrating police enforcement efforts. Two of the five trials took place in Minneapolis, Minnesota; two in Jersey City, New Jersey; and one in Kansas City. The results of the analysis include: Four of five evaluations reported noteworthy crime and disorder reductions; in the two studies that measured crime displacement, shifts were found to be very limited; finally, hot spots policing programs had unintended crime prevention benefits. But the metastudy concludes that the overall results provide "little insight" into the kinds of policing strategies that are most effective: The "small body" of research analyzed does not "unravel the important question of whether enforcement-oriented programs result in long-term crime reductions in hot spot areas," the researchers wrote.

Building on that 2005 research, a 2012 metastudy published in *Justice Quarterly*, "The Effects of Hot Spots Policing on Crime: An Updated Systematic Review and Meta-Analysis," updates the prior findings and provides a more definitive look at the scholarship over the decades by searching through more than 4,000 studies on the topic and identifying the 19 most rigorous. The researchers were Andrew V. Papachristos of Yale, David M. Hureau of Harvard and Anthony Braga of Rutgers (who authored the prior metastudy in 2005); all of the scholars were also affiliated with the Program in Criminal Justice Policy and Management at Harvard Kennedy School. Seventeen of the 19 the studies looked at policing programs in the United States, and 10 were randomized control studies, the gold standard for research.

The findings include:

- Despite more than a decade of improved research methods and analysis, there are still significant uncer-tainties: "Hot spots policing programs generate modest crime control gains and are likely to produce a diffusion of crime control benefits into areas immediately sur-rounding targeted high-activity crime places."

- However, some insights emerge that appear to have scientific validity and practical application. The findings "make a new and very important substantive contribution to crime control theory and practice by identifying problem-oriented policing as a preferable strategy for reducing crime in hot spot locations. Relative to simply increasing police visibility and making additional arrests in crime hot spots, problem-oriented interventions that attempted to alter place characteristics and dynamics produced larger crime prevention benefits."

- Further research must take better account, the scholars note, of those arrested and detained as a result of increased police presence and activity: "Short-term crime gains produced by particular types of hot spots policing initiatives could undermine the long-term stability of specific neighborhoods through the increased involvement of mostly low-income minority men in the criminal justice system." (The scholars point to the findings of a 2008 study in the journal *Criminology* titled "Targeted Enforcement and Adverse System Side Effects: The Generation of Fugitives in Philadelphia.")

"The potential impacts of hot spots policing on police-community relations may depend in good part on the context of the hot spots affected and the types of strategies used," the authors conclude. "An increased enforcement program to control a repeat shoplifting problem in a shopping mall, for instance, may be welcomed by store owners and legitimate customers alike. However, police actions that seek to prevent crime by changing places, such as problem-oriented policing interventions, seem better positioned to generate both crime control gains and positive community perceptions of the police relative to simply increasing police presence and arresting large numbers of offenders."

The researchers also mention that more studies need to focus on the economics of policing strategies and to perform cost/benefit analyses. A related 2013 study, "Could Innovations in Policing Have Contributed to the New York City Crime Drop even in a Period of Declining Police Strength? The Case of Stop, Question and Frisk as a Hot Spots Policing Strategy," examines New York's controversial crime-fighting strategy and how it was executed even as law enforcement resources declined. A study published the same year in the *Annual Review of Economics*, "Deterrence: A Review of the Evidence by a Criminologist for Economists," looks at outcomes for different kinds of policing, arrest, sentencing and punitive strategies.

Related research: As computer analytics software has improved, policing has become more data-driven in some cities, giving rise to "predictive policing." Cities such as Los Angeles have harnessed the power of "Big Data"; in Memphis, police have created programs such as the Blue CRUSH (Crime Reduction Using Statistical History). The National Institute of Justice has held conferences exploring the potential of these new techniques. For more, also see "Reducing Crime through Prevention Not Incarceration," published in *Criminology & Public Policy*, and "Predictive Policing: What Can We Learn from Wal-Mart and Amazon about Fighting Crime in a Recession?"

1. What reasons could account for crime being concentrated in a single neighborhood or area?

2. Besides the idea of predictive policing, what other steps could local governments take to reduce the amount of crime in these "hot spots"? Which do you think would be most effective and why?

EXCERPT FROM "TESTING A CRIME CONTROL MODEL: DOES STRATEGIC AND DIRECTED DEPLOYMENT OF POLICE OFFICERS LEAD TO LOWER CRIME?" BY JAMES P. MCELVAIN, AUGUSTINE J. KPOSOWA, AND BRIAN C. GRAY, FROM THE *JOURNAL OF CRIMINOLOGY*, OCTOBER 8, 2012

ABSTRACT

The purpose of the paper was to investigate whether implementation of a crime control model (based, in part, on the concepts of COMPSTAT) in one southern California city was effective in reducing crime. Time series regression models were fitted to data collected from the Riverside County Sheriff's Department, city of Perris, for the years 2000 through 2010. Additional data were collected from three other cities that served as controls. Results showed that the program was effective in reducing crime rates in Perris. The effect remained significant even after taking into account time trends and control cities. Analysis also found that while the program was more effective in lessening total and property crime rates, it was less so for violent crime rates. It was concluded that strategic and directed policing models (e.g., COMPSTAT, hot spot policing, etc.) may be more effective in crime reduction efforts than reactive policing methods.

1. INTRODUCTION

Throughout the history of law enforcement in the United States, the manner in which service has been delivered continues to be a tremendous challenge to overcome. It seems that from one generation to the next, police departments, whether through self-direction or external pressures, have been tasked with managing personnel in such a manner in order to continue to meet a given community's needs, objectives, problems, and directions despite the level of resources made available to them. Typically, each era of policing has come about as a matter of evolution, or what is generally called a period of "reform," in response to a community's expectation of the service being provided. If each generation of reform were to be viewed as a paradigm, the movement from one paradigm to another could be referred to as a "paradigm shift," fueled by a "continued demand for safer, more effective and efficient ways to police communities" ([1], p.53). The purpose of this paper was to investigate whether the introduction of a crime-control model (based in part on the concepts of COMPSTAT) in one southern California city was effective in reducing crime.

2. PARADIGMS OF POLICING—SHIFTING TO A NEW MODEL

One of the first paradigm shifts followed on the heels of political influence and police corruption, which came about in the middle of the 20th century [1–6]. This "professional" model of policing is also recognized as the "rational-legal bureaucratic" model, which valued a centralized and bureaucratic command structure [1]. During the "professional" era, the primary principles associated with this model were the development of technical skills, training, education, and adherence to the role of crime fighting [6]. Measurement for success was nested in crime statistics such as the number of arrests and response times. Officers were expected to gather "just the facts" and patrol their beats in a random fashion between calls for service as a means to deter criminal conduct.

Given the era and circumstances within the communities and demands on policing, the professional model worked. Between the mid-1900s and into the 1980s our social environment changed, expectations evolved, and, in turn, so did the delivery of police services. In 1968, the President's Commission on Disorder "urged law enforcement to repair its relationship with minority populations and other special interests groups and to "humanize" the behavior of police officers" ([4], p. 70). As a result, policing eventually evolved into what is known as the "community-oriented-policing" era, which did not happen immediately or whole-heartedly by all law enforcement agencies. Some have maintained that community-oriented policing is more talk than action, ineffective, and a mere philosophy that has failed to be actualized by many departments [1, 7–10].

Whether police departments embraced the idea of community-oriented policing or not, there was certainly a demand for a higher, more personalized, level of service by the citizens being served. As a summary of this demand and what the expectation looks like at its optimum level of implementation, Walsh and Vito ([1], p. 55) write, "... in its most ideal form, community policing posits that each community or neighborhood area should be policed in accordance with neighborhood needs and values." In other words, each community would receive a personalized delivery of service wherein beat officers cater to the community's crime and quality of life problems as identified by the community itself. For this to occur, officers need to become intimately familiar with the community, neighborhood, business district, and/or enclave he/she patrols on a daily basis.

Despite its political correctness and feel-good collaborative components, community-oriented policing fell short of its overall expectation. Many departments, at best, implemented a watered-down version [7], which proved to be ineffective. For other departments, it became a philosophy that was spoken in public, but never truly translated to action beyond the level of a subunit (e.g., problem-oriented or special enforcement team) of the department[1]. Moreover, one of the greatest weaknesses in this model of policing is due to its strategy, which is "dependent on the lowest, often less experienced members of the police department who are ill prepared to address complex community problems" ([1], p. 57). While crime rates remained high, public fear of victimization continued, and an overall sense that the quality of life in many communities remained low, a new era in policing was developing.

In their analysis of eight cities that implemented community policing programs, Sadd and Grinc [11] found several challenges that limited the success of this innovative style of policing. In part, the difficulties discovered were internal to the culture and perception of the police officers, whereas others were due to external community forces. These challenges included officers' resistance to change, their possession of only an elementary understanding of the principles of community policing despite efforts to train them, and their failure to see how this was related to "real" police work. Commenting on the officers' perception that community policing was another "politically driven" fad, Sadd and Grinc ([11], p. 11) state, "Some took comfort from the fact that a long list of new projects and restructurings had come and gone without significantly changing the way policing is performed." Essentially, there was a lack of acceptance by the officers, and their pessimistic view of community policing was that community policing was not novel, but repackaged the principles of "good, old-fashioned policing" (p. 11). From the perspective of the community, Sadd and Grinc [11] learned that those neighborhoods that could benefit most from the program (i.e., people living in public housing or underprivileged communities) knew little about community policing beyond "picnics, block parties and events for children" (p. 12). Moreover, like those officers who saw community policing as a phase that would soon pass, community members also held a similar point of view and "define community policing as "just another program" in which services are here today but gone tomorrow" ([11], p. 13).

In spite of the efforts made by law enforcement departments in the past, most continue to struggle with an accurate understanding of crime in our society, and more importantly, they fail to recognize their role. Although this paper addresses contemporary issues facing law enforcement, we suggest that the issue is law enforcement's inability, inefficiency to keep pace with emerging best practices, or unwillingness to recognize its responsibility to do everything in its power to provide the best level of service to reduce crime in our communities. Until law enforcement actually embraces this role, its delivery of service will forever remain an existing issue.

3. THE EMERGENCE OF THE CRIME-CONTROL MODEL

For some time now, many academics and police practitioners have believed that the police could not control crime [4, 7, 8, 12]. There are simply too many social forces that cause criminal behavior for the police to have a direct impact. Some naïveté has given way to more recent research and results from the emerging trend in law enforcement. It should be noted that our use of the term "emerging trend" is a loose interpretation because the concept and development of this latest paradigm shift began more than 17 years ago, but is still finding its way into police departments, big and small, across the United States.

Some researchers assert that crime is caused by poverty, racism and economic injustices [13], economic, social, demographic, and ethnographic forces [7], and/or "… social issues, such as poverty, drugs, and unemployment" ([4], p. 3). Explaining why it was believed that the police could not impact crime, McDonald ([4], p. 3) further states, "Police functioned using traditional enforcement methods of arrest, with the belief that although they could impact individual crime patterns through the arrest of an individual, for the most part they were handicapped in being able to change the flow of crime." In spite of this perspective, and with very little empirical evidence, several police executives have taken credit for crime decreases as a result of their policing practices [14]. In their research, Rosenfeld et al. [8] noted that not all administrators are quick to claim credit for a decrease in crime. The more cautious executives recognize they will eventually be called upon to explain the increases as well.

While serving as the New York City Police Department Commissioner in the early 1990s, William Bratton set out to implement an innovative strategy for policing. Unlike most of the academics and police managers, Bratton believed that, if done right, the police do impact crime; however, they have been going about it the wrong way. By way of the traditional (i.e., professional) model of policing, which arguably continued into the community-oriented policing era, police primarily operated by following the three Rs of policing: rapid response, random patrols, and reactive investigations [1, 4, 7, 15]. Through research, it was observed that random patrol, which was thought to deter crime, merely produced random results [4]. In part, the Kansas City preventive patrol experiment (Kelling et al., [16]) determined that police resources could be better utilized if dedicated to directed crime control strategies as opposed to following the principle of the three Rs. Ultimately, by themselves, the three Rs have demonstrated a failure to effectively prevent or reduce crime, which is the primary, yet often forgotten, mission and responsibility of the police.

Asserting that police had lost sight of their primary role, Bratton and Malinowski ([7], p. 261) state, "... we were encouraged to focus on response to crime and to measure our success by arrest numbers, clearance rates and response time. In effect, we were not held accountable for doing anything to prevent crime." Bratton believed that the "quickest way to impact crime is with a well-led, managed and appropriately resourced police force that embraces risk taking and not risk adversity and a policing structure that includes accountability-focused... management principles..." ([7], p. 261). In order to bring about this change in the delivery of service to coincide with the idea that law enforcement can directly impact and reduce crime Bratton developed a "crime control" model, which is more commonly recognized as "COMPSTAT."

COMPSTAT brings about a change in policing by embracing and incorporating some of the more effective strategies found in both the professional and community-oriented policing models. The basis of the crime control model is premised "on the principle that by controlling serious crime, police are better poised to maintain control and solve other community problems in the promotion of public safety" ([4], p. 1).

4. PRINCIPLES OF COMPSTAT

Declared an innovative approach to policing, which continues to spread across the United States in both large and small law enforcement departments, the crime control model is based on five principles: specific objectives, timely and accurate intelligence, effective strategies and tactics, rapid deployment of personnel and resources, and relentless followup and assessment [4]. (Other researchers provide for as few as four and as many as six principles or strategies (e.g., see [1, 8, 10, 17]).) Each of these principles lends themselves to a significantly different way of operating for any police department that continues to employ the professional or community-oriented policing models. As such, resistance to change can and will occur, especially with managers, those who are impacted at a greater level with this model [18] Bratton believed that he would gain support for organizational change if there was a sense of "internal crisis" shared with the employees [19]. Quoting Bratton, Long et al. ([19], p. 49) write the following:

> Organizations can change the most when they are in crises. When I came to the New York Transit police, it was clear to everyone that the department was in crisis, with crime escalating and morale very low. With the NYPD, we had to create a crisis since there was no crisis of confidence. The prevailing view was that we did things well. We are the best. There is no one any better. So the strategies and reengineering process was intended to create a crisis and process to move the organization through changes... It was revolutionary.

In order to reduce and prevent crime (i.e., the crisis at hand), Bratton instituted a set of management strategies that followed the five principles previously introduced.

One of the shortcomings of community-oriented policing was a lack *of specific objectives.* Specific objectives such as "decreasing street robberies, youth homicide, drug sales to juveniles, vandalism…" by a set percentage of overall crime sends a "powerful message" to those tasked with carrying out the job ([4], p. 8). *Accurate and timely intelligence* is key to directing resources where and when crime occurs. Researchers have come to recognize that crime tends to occur in trends in both time and space, which are identified as "hot spots." This means that by collecting, analyzing and disseminating crime data in a timely manner, police officers can be deployed more effectively, which is the rationalization of policing [17]. Crime data and communication amongst principal enforcers is important to understanding how officers need to respond to emerging problems before they grow or lead to further victimization.

The purpose for collecting and analyzing crime data is to create a clear understanding of the problem. With this information in hand, officers can then develop *effective tactics and strategic responses* to the problem. Departing from the professional and community-oriented policing models, a defined level of accountability is injected into the crime control model. Police managers are empowered (i.e., decentralized decision making) to run their commands all the while maintaining responsibility for results, which tie back into the *specific objectives* we began with. Accountability within this model occurs through executive oversight by the department head or designee, who reviews crime data, patterns of rises and declines in crime, with the managers on a regular basis to ensure that managers are on track with an appropriate level of understanding of the problem and are effectively addressing it. The reason managers are held accountable is because "they have the ability to allocate resources to make effective tactics a reality" ([8], p. 76).

Rapid deployment of personnel and resources and relentless followup and assessment coincide with management accountability and data analysis. The objective is to respond to crime and varying trends as they occur. This means that as crime is mapped geographically as close to real time as possible, managers are encouraged to put the "cops on the dots." This should occur on a regular (i.e., weekly to biweekly) basis "because crime is dynamic and trends emerge and dissipate quickly," which can be as a result of the tactics being employed by the officers [20]. (The frequency of analysis may depend on the amount of available information that would add value to the analysis (i.e., number of reported crimes, calls for service, department size, etc.) To be meaningful, there needs to be something to analyze.) Typically, law enforcement managers skip the process of "assessing and evaluating strategies and tactics" used ([4], p. 21). As a result, they remain uninformed as to what did or did not work. *Relentless followup and assessment* ensures accountability and responsibility on the part of the managers and their staff.

5. CRIME IN TIME AND SPACE

Currently, there is little empirical research supporting a link between COMPSTAT, crime reduction and crime displacement. A common assertion found in the literature was that New York City's remarkable decline in crime, without the occurrence of crime displacement to another location, was attributable to COMPSTAT. Commenting on New York City Police Department's implementation of COMPSTAT, Henry ([21], p. 45) states, "no displacement effect occurred—as reflected in the city-wide statistics, overall crime declined dramatically in every one of the agency's seventy-six precincts, and the greatest percentage decreases were found in precincts where the levels of crime and public disorder were the highest."

In review of crime statistics, mapping, and our own personal experiences, most people recognize that crime does not occur evenly throughout our communities. Relying upon the theory of routine activities, we find that for crime to occur, three things need to take place in time and space: first, there needs to be a motivated person to commit crime; second, a suitable target needs to be present; third, there are no capable guardians present to prevent the criminal act from occurring [22]. Nested in the theory is the idea that based upon routine activities, criminal opportunities rise and fall. Using this theoretical framework, researchers have set out to examine the impact of "hot spot policing" on criminal activity [23]. These researchers were interested in whether a displacement effect (i.e., whether crime simply moves around the corner) occurred as a result of policing tactics.

This particular study is of specific interest in that it empirically tests principles of the crime control model. In their study, Weisburd et al. [23] focus on prostitution and drug sales in two different neighborhoods wherein police crime prevention tactics and strategies were directed in those neighborhoods. In the end, the researchers not only discovered that the targeted criminal activity decreased, it was not displaced to any other nearby location. Moreover, they learned that the policing efforts had a diffusion effect on crime in surrounding areas. Explaining the lack of displacement, Weisburd et al. [23] found that offenders were not motivated to seek out a different location to continue their criminal activity. Clarifying, the offenders interviewed claimed that it would take too much effort and time, there was no established customer base in a new location, they may be treading on another person's turf, and fear of falling victim to violence. The Weisburd et al. [23] study substantiates the efforts of directed crime prevention as an effective means to control crime without displacing it to another location.

6. THE PERRIS STATION

The Perris Station is one of several patrol stations for the Riverside County Sheriff's Department, located in southern California. In addition to patrolling the unincorporated county area surrounding the station, the Perris Station provides full law enforcement services (e.g., patrol, traffic enforcement (this service is provided to the contracted incorporated cities. The California Highway Patrol provides traffic enforcement and conducts collision investigations for the unincorporated county areas), investigations, special enforcement teams—SET, etc.) to more than 213,000 people and covering approximately 190 square miles. Moreover, this station serves as the Police Department for the incorporated cities of Perris, Menifee, and Canyon Lake.

A review of policing practices prior to 2008 at the Perris Station revealed that patrol operations closely followed the professional model of policing (i.e., reactive policing). Upon closer examination, it became apparent that independently, each unit (i.e., patrol, investigations, traffic, SET) worked fairly well if given a specific task to handle. However, there was little direction beyond responding to calls in a timely manner and investigating crimes after the fact. Furthermore, there was no mechanism in place to share information across or within units. Quite frankly, as a detrimental consequence, there was little effort made to examine emerging crime trends and develop strategies to prevent crime.

To overcome what was arguably a definite shortcoming for delivery of service, in 2008, a strategy, loosely based on the COMPSTAT model, was developed to bridge the gap and establish a means to track crime trends and develop strategies to reduce crime. Staff at the Perris Station established continuity by developing small geographical areas of responsibility (i.e., zones) in which deputies were assigned on a regular basis. In order to limit duplication of effort, and strengthen communication amongst staff members and with other units, a pass-on system for sharing information was devised. This structure ensured that not only did each unit have access to developing trends within a geographical area, but each person assigned to this same area, despite their assignment, had access as well. In conjunction with the pass-on system, deputies assigned to the special enforcement team (SET) were designated as "zone coordinators." Taking a different accountability approach as established in the COMPSTAT model, wherein station or area commanders (i.e., persons of higher rank) are held accountable for the results, the Perris Station model followed more of a community-oriented policing philosophy (i.e., entrusting more decision-making authority to the line level deputy) by empowering the zone coordinators (rank of deputy) to develop and employ crime prevention strategies.

Each zone coordinator was tasked with ensuring
that crime data (i.e., Part 1 crimes by zone), which was
produced biweekly by the station crime analyst, was
reviewed through a process of "analysis and response" and
provided in a report every two weeks. The report consisted
of detailed crime maps for each zone showing "hot spots,"
tables presenting crime changes over time (i.e., two-week,
year-to-date, etc.), and charts demonstrating trends by
time of day and day of week. The "analysis" section of the
report consisted of describing a particular crime trend for
a given crime category such as burglary (e.g., what was
occurring-method of operation used by the suspect, simi-
larity among victims, locations and times, who the suspects
were if identified, etc.). The "response" section outlined
what action was to be taken to minimize or prevent the
crime pattern from continuing. Overtime, the analysis and
response sections became more refined so as to provide
clear direction to the end user (e.g., identifying for the
patrol officer assigned to a specific zone the locations to
patrol, timeframe in which the criminal activity was occurring, suspects to look for, etc.).

The deputies assigned as the zone coordinators, by
way of their assignment, assume much of the responsibility
in this model; however, they are provided great freedom to
adjust their work schedules as new crime trends emerge
in their zones. Additionally, accountability for the results
of the crime control strategies used by each zone coordinator is shared amongst their peers, supervisors, the lieutenants and station commander on a biweekly basis. This
is accomplished every other week when the stakeholders
(i.e., zone coordinators, representative patrol deputies,
station supervisors, lieutenants, commander, as well as

members from the Investigations Unit, Traffic Unit, Crime Analysis Unit, Gang Task Force and Narcotics Task Force) meet to review the current crime trends. Each person, specifically the supervisors, lieutenants, and commander, is responsible for being familiar with the current trends, strategies, and tactics being used to address the identified crime problems. Although the zone coordinator assumes most of the responsibility for addressing questions delivered from the station's management team, the environment is not meant to be adversarial or contentious. To share in the overall accountability of the results, the Perris Station model strived to encourage the more experienced participants (i.e., supervisors and managers) to help guide and develop crime reduction strategies and tactics.

One of the challenges to research is gaining access to data and being able to conduct empirical evaluation of the effectiveness of a given program. At present, we have a defined period in time in which the Perris Station altered its policing strategy, which offered an opportunity for evaluation. As stated earlier, the purpose of this study was to determine whether the crime control model that was developed at the Perris Station was effective in reducing crime rates. The study also compares crime rates in Perris to three other cities that did not use such crime control methods. Using the city of Perris as our test case, it is our hypothesis that the crime control model, with its proactive crime prevention strategies and techniques, supports reduction of Part 1 crime (e.g., homicide, robbery, rape, assault, burglary, autotheft, larceny, and arson) as a whole when compared to three control cities (Lake Elsinore, Coachella, and La Quinta).

[...]

9. DISCUSSION

As other researchers have pointed out, there is little empirical research on COMPSTAT or other similar crime control models [17]. The authors point out "those studies that do exist tend to be brief, rely heavily on anecdotal evidence, or concentrate on the nation's largest, and, by any measure, most exceptional police department, the NYPD" (p. 465). In fact, with few exceptions, much that is written tends to describe the principles and methods behind the COMPSTAT model as opposed to testing the effectiveness of the model by comparing crime data before and after implementation of the conceptual polic-ing model or testing it against controls (i.e., comparable cities that did not employ the same policing strategy). In one case in which researchers examined the effects of COMPSTAT on New York City homicides, they found no significant change in reported incidents when compared to other cities [14] despite other researchers claiming evidence that the COMPSTAT model of policing reduced violent crime in New York City [29]. Furthermore, in another location and under different circumstances, but exploring the effectiveness of a version of the crime control model, other researchers found that when the police employ well-defined crime prevention strategies and tactics, they experienced a reduction in crime with no evidence of displacement [30].

Given the few number of empirical studies that examine whether the crime control model effectively does what it conceptually claims to do, the present study was undertaken to investigate the effectiveness of the crime control model as implemented at the Riverside County

Sheriff's Department, Perris Station, in the city of Perris and compared to three control cities. Here, we would note that it should be generally understood that that every law enforcement agency would commonly have within their mission to minimize crime; however, the manner in which a police department goes about doing so may depend on management philosophy, resources, and knowledge of best practices.

While crime trends may have been decreasing for some of the cities in this study prior to 2008 (Perris being one of them), evidence indicates that the crime control model, as applied in the city of Perris, accelerated the crime decrease in the subsequent years. Because of the prior trend, it would be overly optimistic, without further analysis and evidence, to assert that the crime control model caused the decrease in the following years. However, relying collectively upon several factors, one can deduce that there is a relationship between the enhanced crime decrease and the policing strategies employed in the city of Perris. First, when examining the crime trends over time [...], we find that Perris and Lake Elsinore were the only cities to experience a crime rate decrease for total, violent and property crimes during the 11-year period; Coachella's total and property crime rates increased (we acknowledge that the increase in property crime rate is simultaneously inflating the total crime rate here), and the violent crime rate rose in the city of La Quinta. Further, when comparing the decrease in crime rates for Perris and Lake Elsinore, the rate of decrease was greatest for Perris across each crime category. Respectively, the crime rate decreased in Perris 45 percent, 53 percent, and 43 percent for total, violent, and property crimes, whereas the decrease in Lake Elsinore was 19 percent, 49 percent, and 13 percent.

[...] It was found that the crime rates declined substantially in the years following the implementation of the crime control model. Even after controlling for other cities that did not introduce the program [...], it was observed that years following the execution of the model in Perris still showed reduction of total crime rates.

Analysis also showed that perhaps researchers investigating program effectiveness (e.g., COMPSTAT) need to disaggregate crimes by specific types. We found that in Perris, while the program worked for total and property crimes, it was less effective with regard to violent crimes [...]. Before definitive conclusions can be drawn, given the fact that the coefficients were all in the negative direction, there is evidence to suggest that programs such as the one evaluated in this study may become more effective with time.

Despite the value of this study, there were some limitations. The first limitation was briefly discussed above regarding the short duration of time in which the model has been operating. Under better circumstances, we would have more data (i.e., years) to examine; however, as is the nature with examining the effectiveness of various programs, time might not always work in favor of the research. In the end, we need to take advantage of each research opportunity as they arise and make the best of them.

Another limitation was that despite our best effort to make a cautious comparison with other similar cities, it was difficult to provide a direct assessment of crime differences or similarities because each city tends to be diverse in a number of ways that make such a comparison nearly impossible, if not impractical. In fact, the FBI cautions against making this type of comparison [31]. Thus, to attribute any decreases in crime to one factor such as the implementation of a specified crime control program would be overreaching. Ideally, we would have liked to have had more control variables in the analysis such as unemployment, household size, state and local economic performance and more specific population demographics, but such data were not available. Even if they were, the sample size for each city was limited.

A third limitation to the study lies within the complexity of the crime control model itself. While we maintain that our analysis indicated that the crime control strategies developed in Perris accelerated the crime decrease in the city as compared to the control cities, more research is necessary to more narrowly define what it is about the model that is most effective. Notwithstanding what we have learned in the present study, much remains unknown. To still be determined is what specific component found within the crime control model produced or contributed to the crime decline experienced in Perris. Could it be the data collection and analysis, the accountability and ownership of a geographic area by the zone coordinator deputies, the strategic review process with police administration and line-level stakeholders, or some combination of strategies? Further research could help answer this question and prove informative to police agencies interested in implementing a similar program.

In spite of the limitations observed above, findings support the argument that the manner in which police officers are deployed matters (i.e., the implemented crime control model in Perris); police can be more effective when their efforts are strategically directed at identified crime trends.

Although it can be argued that any type of policing reform implemented at the Perris Station could have resulted in a decrease in crime, this study focused on a specific model. As such, our study adds to the research that the police, as demonstrated through the benefits of the crime control model, can in fact reduce and prevent crime based on the model's principles of gathering and tracking current crime data, sharing information, and employing strategic policing methods. Analyses provide evidence to suggest that strategic policing models (e.g., COMPSTAT, hot spot policing, etc.) may be more effective than reactive policing methods. In an ever diminishing environment for police funding, police departments may find value by investing in a crime control model as opposed to employing the principles of the professional model, which is based on rapid response, random patrols, and reactive investigations.

1. After reading this study, do you think the crime control model presented by the researchers is one that can be replicated and used in other cities? Why or why not?

2. The researchers note that police procedures need to be updated as our society changes. What updates would you suggest to work best with our current culture? How do you think your updates would change things?

EXCERPT FROM *ETHICS IN LAW ENFORCEMENT*, BY STEVE MCCARTNEY AND RICK PARENT

7.6 TRANSACTIONAL AND TRANSFORMATIONAL LEADERSHIP

Huberts, Kaptein, and Lasthuizen (2007) found that effective role modelling is especially significant in demonstrating moral behaviour, while strictness is especially effective in limiting fraud, corruption, and the misuse of resources. As an extension of strictness, the ethics of law enforcement agencies are likely to be greater when there are rules, regulations, and systems of oversight that carefully manage law enforcement behaviour. In the case of law enforcement agencies, the behaviour usually occurs on the street, where street police officers are interacting with civilians without supervision. Because the police are out of view and not supervised for much of their working day, leadership must evolve away from strictness as a way to promote ethical conduct.

There are two distinct models of leadership that operate within large organizations: transformational and transactional. Historically, due to the paramilitary nature of law enforcement, leadership has largely been transactional. **Transactional leadership** in law enforcement is a style of management used by those who are more oriented toward bureaucracy and maintaining the status quo. Transactional leaders tend to take the decision-making powers away from those they supervise and to make decisions on their own, not yielding power to those beneath them in the hierarchy. This leadership style often runs contrary to what is practised in law enforcement: the requirement to exercise discretion throughout the ranks (Bass, 1990).

Bowie (2000) asserts that leadership is not effective unless managers empower subordinates to make decisions; however, the empowerment of subordinates is at odds with the military hierarchical system. What is required is a system that allows subordinates to make operational decisions and leadership that is willing to risk the mistakes that result from these decisions. Mastrofski (2004) suggests the way to achieve these goals is through **transformational leadership**, which guides officers to make the right decisions by following the moral lead of their managers who possess the moral standards that are shared by the organization. Failure to promote these values will lead subordinates to mirror the unethical practices of their leader, resulting in poor decisions. There are risks associated in allowing subordinates to use discretion, such as forgetting, missing, or just not adhering to the morals of their leader; risk is unavoidable when subordinates are given increased discretion.

The risk of poor decisions at the operational level requires strong leadership in which managers not only understand the risk but also are willing and able to bear the weight of this risk (Villiers, 2003). Such a style of leadership is difficult within a culture that is so deeply entrenched in a military type of structure, where following policy and rules are expected throughout the hierarchy. Villiers (2003, p. 28) describes this as "mechanistic bureaucratization" in which the policing service operates in an autocratic style, which is contrary to the autonomy police officers have in exercising their discretion. Villiers (2003) further argues that a more democratic style of leadership is required in order to effectively lead the officer who exercises more discretion than his or her manager.

Transformational leadership is conducive to discretionary policing and, in its purest form, empowers subordinates to make moral decisions that are reflective of the organization (Bass, 1990). The transformational leader requires followers to transcend their own interests to uphold the interests of the organization by focusing on future and long-term goals instead of short-term satisfaction (Bass, 1990). A transformational leader is required to exert his or her organizational morals on subordinates who will in turn make decisions that reflect the leader's values and therefore the organization's values. The result of such effective leadership is a subordinate who, when confronted with operational decisions, will be able to make the same decisions that his or her leader would make. In this way, a transformational leader is a "developer of people and a builder of teams who inspire their followers to act and make decisions" (Bass, 1990, p.54). Bass (1990) further describes those that possess such qualities as being naturally gifted and suggests that one is either born with the trait or not, which renders them a valuable commodity.

The notion that transformational leaders are born, not made, presents a problem for law enforcement agencies that need sergeants and other managers to possess both operational knowledge and transformational qualities. The possibility that managers cannot be taught transformational qualities potentially eliminates those who hold only operational knowledge as an attribute. Tourish, Craig, and Amernic (2010, p.41) describe such leaders as "exceptional people" who are also powerful and have the ability to understand organizational values as well as the personalities of their followers. Police managers, having risen through the ranks, may or may not be capable of developing such attributes and as result, require training. In their qualitative study of managers, Hay and Hodgkinson (2006) found managers who felt that training in these qualities is a difficult prospect and something that cannot be learned in courses. This makes it difficult for those police managers who are not born with these qualities to learn and apply them on a regular basis. Courses in leadership are used to train officers of all ranks; however, there have been few studies that have determined whether this training leads to transformational leadership or not. The question remains: can competent operational officers learn the skills to be transformational leaders?

The notion of transformational leadership in policing is sometimes at odds with police culture for the following reasons:

- Officers are unlikely to embrace the transformational leader due to their inculcation in the blame culture where blame is assessed when discretion has failed and a mistake is made (Villiers, 2003). The blame culture is a double-edged sword:
    - First, operational officers mistrust their superiors, believing that if they make a mistake, they will be held accountable.
    - Second, managers have difficultly extricating themselves from the blame culture when assessing the poor discretionary decision of a subordinate.
- Police culture is generally characterized by cynicism toward leadership, and this is especially true toward

leaders who are charismatic and are purveyors of transformational leadership values (Villiers, 2003).

- Transformational leaders must fight the blame culture and be willing to accept the inevitable risk associated with decisions made at the operational level. As discretion increases, so too does the risk of more mistakes. The manager who assumes the role of transformational leader must accept this risk as a part of officers' development rather than as an opportunity to blame.

- In acknowledging the inevitability of discretion, Mastrofski (2004) maps out transformational leadership as the best way to ensure proper and effective control of discretion among operational police officers. Transformational leadership convinces officers to make the right discretionary choices by persuading them to achieve the right goals without the need to directly supervise them. Officers functioning beyond the view of their superiors will need to use discretion, and if they have adopted the values of their leader (and therefore their organization), they will likely make decisions that are based on these shared values (Bass, 1990).

1. Which of the two leadership styles presented in this section do you think is one that may lead critics to claim police are trained to use excessive force? Why is that?

2. Are both leadership styles just as likely to result in practices that may cause harm to suspects? Why or why not?

EXCERPT FROM "DIVERSITY IN THE BRITISH POLICE: ADAPTING TO A MULTICULTURAL SOCIETY," BY BELA BHUGOWANDEEN, FROM *CAHIERS DU MIMMOC*, OCTOBER 2013

INTRODUCTION

The police force has long been stigmatised in Britain as far as race relations are concerned. After the Race Relations Act of 1976[1], the procedures for recruiting police officers underwent two major overhauls in the 1980s and early 2000s following official inquiries sparked by the 1982 urban disturbances and a botched police investigation into a racist murder. Historically white male dominated, the police service was criticised for having a sexist and racist culture and lacking black, Asian and female officers. Research influenced by the cultural studies school from the mid-1970s[2] revealed disproportionate targeting of minority groups and racist stereotyping[3].

The low numbers of ethnic minorities in the police service and other public institutions was highlighted in 1999 with the publication of the Macpherson Report into the Inquiry following Stephen Lawrence's murder. The Race Relations Act of 2000[4] reinforced public authorities' duties to prevent racial discrimination, promote racial equality and promote good relations between members of different racial groups. All 43 police forces in England and Wales were required to meet targets set by the government to increase the number of recruits from minority ethnic communities. These targets vary from region to region set according to the make-up of the ethnic population in each region. The National Target set in 1999 to reflect the national average 7% ethnic minority population in England and Wales was 7% ethnic minority officers by 2009. However, in 2012, it was reported that "The proportion of police officers that consider themselves to be from a minority ethnic background has risen from under 2% in 1997 to 5%."[5] This paper examines the nature and extent of the changes in recruitment and training of police made between 1995 and 2005 and examines the reasons for its relative success drawing on interviews with Thames Valley Police officers and staff in 2007.

THE MOVE TOWARDS DIVERSITY

The Race Relations Act 2000 imposes specific duties on all public authorities in the UK in terms of recommendations for those public authorities concerned to make sure that they execute the general duties imposed by the Act. It required public authorities in England and Wales to produce and publish a Racial Equality Scheme (RES) for the police service or Racial Equality Policy (REP) for schools and other public authorities.

To make sure that their equality policies were working, a process of ethnic monitoring[6] was established collecting general statistics on employees' ethnic backgrounds to see if equality of opportunity is achieved by all ethnic groups. The Commission for Racial Equality (CRE)[7] is able to take action over non compliance[8].

Since the Lawrence Inquiry Report of February 1999 on police failings in the investigation into the murder of Stephen Lawrence in 1993, awareness of the notion of 'diversity' in the police force recognised that the provision of a service designed for the white majority ethnic population no longer worked. Diversity initiatives have been developed in forces around England and Wales in order to promote awareness of racial issues and discrimination, change police officers' behaviour and attitudes and reinforce relationships with local minority communities. It was also intended to change the image of the police force into that of a precursor of diversity initiatives thus attracting a wider range of entrants into the force.

The new internal approach in terms of training focused on and revolved around what has been described as 'race relations awareness' or 'community and race relations awareness'.

Traditional training for police officers had been the provision of information about the law and police procedures but there was nothing about the role of officers in society and what society expected from them. Would-be officers were not aware that a diverse society had different cultures and traditions with diverse demands which had to be dealt with differently. In fact they were not really well prepared to face the problems that communities or they themselves would encounter. Though Community Race Relations training did exist in the early 1970s, it lacked specifics on dealing with ethnic minorities.

In his report (1986) on the causes for the 1982 riots in Brixton, a district with a large Afro-Caribbean population, Lord Scarman appealed for the reform of police training and recommended training in community relations.

> The training of police officers must prepare them for policing a multi-racial society. [...] the present training arrangements are inadequate. [...] inadequate emphasis is put in training on the problems

of policing a multi-racial society. More attention should therefore be devoted, it was suggested, to the training of police officers in, for example the understanding of the cultural background of ethnic minority groups and in the stopping of people in the street.[9] (Scarman 5.16)

Training courses designed to develop the understanding that good community relations are not merely necessary but are essential to good policing should, I recommend, be compulsory from time to time in a police officer's career up to and including the rank of Superintendent.[10] (Scarman 5.28)

The existing training provisions were reviewed in response to Scarman's proposals. However, few forces had systematically included race relations training within their policies and practices.

The Scarman Report had given direction but issued no requirements, whereas the Macpherson Report (1999) into the Lawrence murder inquiry, instigated a wide ranging review of police training in terms of diversity and racism:

That there should be an immediate review and revision of racism awareness training within Police Services to ensure [...] that training courses are designed and delivered in order to develop the full understanding that good community relations are essential to good policing and that a racist officer is a incompetent officer.[11] (Recommendation 48)

It also recommended that these be monitored and measured in terms of their implementation and effectiveness (Recommendation 53) : all police officers but also civilian staff "should be trained in racism awareness and valuing cultural diversity" (Recommendation 49)

Like other forces in the England and Wales, the Thames Valley Police is doing its best to recruit more and more Black and Minority Ethnics in order to meet the targets set by government, efforts which are considered to promote diversity, and improve race relations within the force and within communities. [...]

The total number of recruits had more than doubled after two years with 190 officers in 1999-2000 and 463 officers in 2002-2003. However, there was only a slight increase in the number of minority ethnics employed. [...] The trend is barely visible for ethnic minorities despite the increase in total number of officers recruited during those years. This can partly be explained by the nega- tive impact of the Macpherson report in 1999 on police forces in general and attitudes of ethnic minorities to seek a career in the police service. The number of ethnic minority police officers recruited within the Thames Valley Police remained low in 2005-2006. Certain categories was very poorly represented (Any Other Asian, Any Other Black, Any Other Mixed, Black Caribbean and Pakistani), despite there beinn a large Indian and Black Caribbean community in the area. The low number of Bangladeshis in the Thames Valley area reported in the 2001 census explains why Bangladeshis are not represented in the four charts above [12].

The Thames Valley Police therefore continued to face under representation of ethnic minorities at a time when 40% of the population in Slough was from minority ethnic communities, predominantly Asian[13]. Despite the fact that Thames Valley Police have their own Race Equality Scheme, as required by the Race Relations Act 2000, reviewed every three years, and a civilian Equality

Schemes Co-ordinator, the force found it difficult to keep pace with and reflect the influx of large numbers of ethnic minority immigrants in towns in their police region. Thames Valley Police have their own Diversity Unit, set up in September 2005 to ensure that all aspects of diversity are promoted[14], a Diversity Board to monitor progress and a Diversity Action Group to drive through action on diversity issues[15]. In order to have a workforce whose composition reflects the communities it serves, the Thames Valley Police have also appointed a team of staff who dedicate their time to recruiting and retaining Black and Minority Ethnics. One of them is the Black and Minority Ethnic (BME) Recruitment Team who makes sure the recruitment of ethnic minorities is made according to the procedures which exist and also to make sure that they get the support they need once they are already in the force.

Furthermore, there is a wide range of staff associations and staff working groups to provide advice and support and help promote diversity and equality within the force[16]. One of the associations working together to improve the working environment of Black Minority Ethnic staff within the Thames Valley Police force, is the Thames Valley Black Police Association, a local version of the National Black Police Association, an initiative put forward in the 1990s when a considerable number of black staff were leaving police forces throughout the UK. A Black Police Association now exists in most police forces around the country. Even if all of these units and associations work towards the promotion of equality of opportunity and diversity, there is a difference between the Diversity Unit and the Thames Valley Black Police

Association or the Black Police Association in general.
The Diversity Unit works on all six strands of diversity
which are race, gender, disability, sexual orientation, faith
and age whereas the Thames Valley Black Police Association concentrates on Black and (other) Minority Ethnics.
At the Thames Valley Police, all new police recruits,
including civilian staff, participate in the compulsory race
and Diversity Training Programme and a Community Relations Programme aimed at ensuring that they have an
understanding of people from different backgrounds.

COMMUNITY AND RACE RELATIONS TRAINING

In response to the Race Relations Act (2000) and the
Marpherson recommendations, Community and Race
Relations training was instituted as a means to make staff
more sensitive to the diverse cultures and experiences
of minority groups. For example, officers would visit the
mosque to learn about Muslim culture and traditions; not
wearing shoes in a mosque for instance. They would be
aware that they should interact differently with men and
women among ethnic minority groups. This would eventually facilitate their work and also strengthen relations
with local communities.

Secondly, the Community Race Relations training was
also aimed at changing officers' attitudes as it was believed
that behaviour inside the force reflected the behaviour of
police officers outside the force when they would interact
with the communities. Indeed, prior to the Stephen Lawrence
Inquiry, discriminatory behaviour and racist, sexist and
homophobic language were commonplace. One senior
interviewee in the Thames Valley Police remarked:

> There is no overt racism I would say. Whether or not there is discrimination it is difficult to measure that. But certainly the culture of the organisation has changed [...] I mean fast forward twenty seven years, no racist abuse at all within the organisation actually. I am not saying racism does not exist, it still exists but it is all underground, people are more subtle about it. (*Interview*)

However the decline in the use of inappropriate language was related to the disciplinary response rather than a changing of attitudes of officers towards racist language.

> But even so, I think racism exists within society so there would be racism within the force as we draw people from society. So some might say it might exist more in the force because of the sort of people attracted to the job. But nobody now would make racist comments as they know they will lose their job. We cannot change attitudes and sometimes it enters the bloodstream of an organisation and it is difficult to detect and we talk about institutional racism actually. (*Interview*)

It appeared to be more difficult to detect who is racist and who is not :

> As ethnic minorities we knew who the racists were within the organisation. [...] There is something very interesting. There is this particular character who racially abused me from the minute I bloody joined up really who later went on to be in charge of recruiting ethnic minorities. In my eyes his heart was not in it at all. (*Interview*)

The awareness training and new disciplinary rules are a way to keep officers abreast of changing accepted terms:

It is a two-sided thing in the UK we have political correctness and sometimes we could be too draconian. Just because somebody says a wrong word, we are not going to jump on them and make an example of them. In 1980, when I joined, it was not uncommon for you to hear people saying there is coloured man there and you thought you were being polite. But now 'coloured' is just not politically correct you just do not use that or else you would offend people. Some people have not caught up with the language. When I was born I was 'half-caste' then 'mixed race' and now I am 'dual-heritage'. So you would have to keep up with the word and just because somebody would say 'half-caste' you won't sack them. (*Interview*)

There is a whole hierarchy of sanctions. There is a management advice where they would tell you not to use that kind of language. 'Things have changed now we don't use that language anymore'. Then there are higher sanctions like written warnings, fine, getting involved in a discipline of caution or you get suspended or sacked. (*Interview*)

Thames Valley Police, Slough in particular, with significant ethnic minority communities, was a good example of forces who had introduced training and awareness to meet individual needs of its staff. Many of the initiatives involved community participation in the training which in itself helped break down stereotypical barriers: "Slough in particular has always been the centre of energy for diversity initiatives within the force." (*Interview*)

Secondly, external approaches were developed to promote diversity in the police force and the trust and confidence of ethnic minority communities. Communities as a whole changed significantly during the decade 1955-2005. Social class was replaced by a growing social and cultural pluralism with a myriad of age, race, religion, gender, sexuality, ethnicity and lifestyles.

The Stephen Lawrence Inquiry report had identified a "[…] striking and escapable need to demonstrate fairness not just by police services but across the criminal justice system as a whole, in order to generate trust and confidence with minority ethnic communities."[17] (Para 46.30) It suggested that "[...] genuine partnership between the police and all section of the community must be developed."[18] (Para 46.40) The Lawrence Report stated categorically that the police must not deliver a service which is "colour blind" but rather one that "recognises the different experiences, perceptions and needs of a diverse society"[19]. (Para 45.24) .

Police consultation with local communities received greater ressources. Liaison officers were introduced to liaise with black and minority ethnic communities and improve communication as a step towards increasing trust and confidence. White minorities are also taken into consideration with police officers learning Polish to facilitate contacts with the large local Polish community in Slough. Prior to these courses in Polish, translators were needed which must have slowed down the process and incurred misunderstandings. Community talks by ethnic minority officers themselves to listen to the communities' demands, reassure the minority population about the police culture and encourage people to join the force. Meetings in schools and community centres were held for people to get used to the presence of police without misapprehension.

Ethnic minority staff often start with an advantage when dealing with ethnic minority communities, which may simply be the perception of an absence of racism or simply language skills, cultural and religious sensitivity and shared common experiences which can be exploited to improve community relations. The senior officer interviewed remarked "they feel that there is a shared common experience that I would have experienced racism as well." As a consequence, "they trust me more than they would do a white cop" as "with a white officer you have to earn the trust first and this might take a bit longer".

A further external approach initiated by the Thames Valley Police praised the need to liaise with communities in response to events which had the potential for 'critical' impact on local communities. A clear example of that were the impact of the terrorist attacks in New York in September 2001. There were a number of racial attacks and abuse in the Slough area following 9/11 and special effort was made to retain the trust and confidence of communities.

> [...] there was a lot of tension. Lots of ethnic minorities, Muslims in particular, but actually all, any non white people were very concerned that there would be a right wing backlash and that they would be picked on and being accused of being the Taliban, Bin Laden that sort of thing. (*Interview*)

The 9/11 attacks on the USA also had an impact on the minority police officers in England and Wales:

> One of the repercussions of that was even ethnic minority cops started to feel a bit concerned that their colleagues would turn on them and say 'wait a second which side are you on? Are you

on the Bin Laden side or one of us?' So for a few weeks there was some anxiety among our ethnic minority cops. (*Interview*)

A Muslim Police Constable officer, explains how he felt post 9/11:

I love what I am doing then the problem of fitting in arose again after 9/11 when your own colleagues start looking at you differently, just because you are a Muslim. Though you have been in the force for a long time and have done a good job you start questioning the trust and confidence. (*Interview*)

Operation Comfort was specifically intended to reassure the community and to deter the far right : "[...] we are getting skin heads coming around targeting things nationally. Wherever there is any conflict the BNP [British National Party] would use that to divide communities." (*Interview*)

[...] after 9/11 we saw an outbreak of disorder in town where Asian people were attacked you know like hijab[20] ripped off people's heads, Sikh men attacked and that sort of stuff. In response to that was 'Operation Comfort', we wanted to try to reassure the community that the police care about the racist attacks. (*Interview*)

This operation in Slough consisted of deploying officers from ethnic minority backgrounds in the streets in an area with large ethnic minority communities. There were only eight of them deployed in the streets of Slough as it seemed that too many officers frightened people. The officers were selected for their ethnic origins, their "high level of awareness of race and discrimination" and " high level of language skills" (*Interview*) .

However, some resentment as to the use of this strategy was felt on the part of some senior officers, as it was considered to be a risky business. Indeed, the feedback from the ethnic minority officers was the opportunity to use their diverse talent. "A few of the black people speaking different languages are being visible and being given a licence to use their language skills and target ethnic minority communities." In fact, there is a perception "when you come into the police you have to forget about all your culture and your heritage and you have to conform, you put a uniform and then you are one of us." (*Interview*) Operation Comfort gave them the opportunity to use their ethnic and cultural inheritance. The operational approach proved to be a success and had a positive impact on the community.

> The community impact as I then followed up this operation with a number of visits to the temples and the mosques. Without exception when I arrived there, I was about to tell them about the black and Asian officers and they told me they already heard about that. They said that there were hundreds of ethnic minority officers everywhere in the streets in Slough. There were not hundreds but only eight assigned. So the impact was such that they thought there were hundreds. They asked 'We didn't know you got so many ethnic minority officers.' (*Interview*)

Ethnic minority officers deployed on this operation were approached and asked questions about the police service:

> 'What is it like in the police then? Are they all racists [...]?' We had some genuine recruiting inquiries and some people joined up purely as a result of that operation. It was a real success' (*Interview*)

This tactic was to be adopted by other police forces during period of heightened tensions.

It had been shown that diversity could be used more effectively to improve the service and that several examples of effective utilisation of diversity held much potential for wider development across police forces. Though there were uncertainties about the use of certain strategies, it was evident that senior officers in other forces recognised the importance of releasing the diverse talent for a positive impact on communities. The Black Police Association was cited as the most important success for ethnic minority staff in terms of opportunities it provided to network with each other.

THE BLACK POLICE ASSOCIATION

The Black Police Association was one of the major initiatives within the police service at a time when it was obvious that the issues of racism and resignation among black police officers were commonplace. Indeed, in the 1990s, ethnic minority officers tolerated racism in order to be accepted by colleagues. Moreover, the Met had difficulties in recruiting and retaining minority officers in the early 1990s. In response to these problems, the first Black Police Association was set up in 1994, by ethnic minority officers and staffs within the Metropolitan Police Service, as a support network that sought to work with the service to improve the working environment of black personnel within the Metropolitan Police. After several years of discussion and planning, the National Black Police Association was created in 1998 and has become a powerful voice within the police service. As a means to foster diversity within the force today, its ultimate goal is help police deliver an equitable service to all sections of the community.

The Thames Valley Black Police Association (TVBPA) was created in 1999 as a direct consequence of the Stephen Lawrence Inquiry "to support ethnic minority staff, police officers staff and civilian staff, to try to get the best out of them, to tell them to reach their potential, to be a supportive network where people can talk about their shared experiences." (*Interview*) Most police forces today have their own Black Police Association to improve the recruitment, retention and development of staff from minority backgrounds. The main reason why police forces needed a supportive network within the force was that ethnic minorities could not talk to each other because they were suspected of plotting.

> We tended not to talk to each other because we thought if we are seen talking to each other as ethnic minorities, the white majority might wonder what we were planning. This sort of validates the networking of ethnic minorities for the first time that it is ok to get together. When we got together for the first time we shared the experiences that we had had as we grew up within the organization and they were very similar though we never talked about it before and you only think it's happening to you as an individual. (*Interview*)

In addition, the networking empowered ethnic minority staff and gave them the opportunity to take their issues to the top of the police service: "We then were able to get to the chief constable and say 'look at our experiences; these are the sort of stuff that we would like to happen'." (*Interview*) The Black Police Association has been often consulted for policy issues since its creation in 1998 on community issues.

The Thames Valley Black Police Association also aimed develop trust and confidence within the community and helped minority staff to promote good relations with ethnic minority communities of the three counties of Berkshire, Buckinghamshire and Oxfordshire. For instance ethnic minority officers were harassed by their own communities for being a police officer and as such 'traitors'. The Black Police Association was the instigator of exercises involving ethnic minority officers patrolling their local area, such as 'Operation Comfort'. As a result of these exercises many young people from minority communities talked about their desire to join the force.

Despite the clearly stated aims of the Thames Valley Black Police Association,, there was some reluctance among the ethnic minority officers to be a member of the association and this is confirmed by Chief Superintendent Brian Langston who chaired the Thames Valley Black Police Association for a number of years:

> So when we created the TVBPA in 1999, there were still a number of people who didn't join it. They saw it as a militant organisation it's all black power and a chip on your shoulder or something like that when it's not like that at all. Why would you want to associate with them you know that sort of thing. (*Interview*)

They were likely to be criticized for leaving their shifts to attend Black Police Association meetings. "The middle management would say 'Yes you can go to your meeting but it leaves us very short on the shift'; and make them feel very guilty about spending time networking with BPA officers." (*Interview*)

Some of the minority officers interviewed expressed reservations about the Thames Valley Black Police Association. Muslim Police Constables were reserved about the Association. One, a member of TVBPA said "But I am not sure about 'Black' Police Association. Why should it be 'black'? What if white officers join the association? What about neutral names for it, as things have moved forward now?"

The same feelings were expressed by a further interviewee.

> I feel that calling it Black Police Association creates confusion for other ethnic minority officers as it could have been called 'Minority Police Association'. There is a misunderstanding about that. [The Macpherson Report] has benefited only one community; that is to say the black community. Problems encountered by ethnic minority officers do not concern only black officers but also Asian officers and all other ethnic minority officers. (*Interview*)

Another ethnic minority Sergeant who joined the Association, also said that there were still not many people joining the association due to apprehension from communities: "It looks too glossy." The former chairman of the Thames Valley Black Police Association felt that it is not as necessary in 2007 as it was in 1999.

THE NUMBERS GAME

The government response to one of the key recommendations of the Macpherson Report into the Stephen Lawrence Inquiry, with the introduction of targets for all police forces in England and Wales, was a step towards the recruitment of more black and minority ethnics in order to reflect the different communities which they served. The introduction of targets had its advantages but also put pressure on some police forces which had difficulties in recruiting minority ethnics. As a result, some of them used illegal methods, like positive discrimination, in order to meet targets at the peril of maintaining standards within the force and relations between officers within the force. Indeed, the Race Relations Act 1976[21] makes it unlawful for a person to discriminate on racial grounds against another in any circumstances.

The Home Office directed each force to meet a target reflecting the racial make-up of its local population by 2009. The same national target for every force would simply have created difficulties for some forces in rural areas where there were few black and Asian people compared to forces in urban areas like London and Birmingham where different ethnic minority communities are concentrated. The Home Office ten year national average target of 7% for minority officers in England and Wales to be reached by 2009. In comparison to other sectors of employment, like the National Health Service or the London Transport for example, the police service remained a white male racist and sexist force. Indeed, the police service is in stark contrast to the other above mentioned employment sectors who have high percentages of ethnic minorities and women employees.

In London, the Metropolitan Police Service (MPS) for instance was given a target of 26 per cent of ethnic minority police officers by 2009 givenLondon's 25 percent minority population. In 2005, the Thames Valley Police force had 2.5 per cent of serving ethnic minority officers[22] for an ethnic minority population of 5.35 per cent.

Target settings seemed to have both its advantages and disadvantages in the promotion of diversity within the police service. On the one hand, the main advantage of targets was that success or failure for the recruitment of officers from minority ethnic backgrounds was clearly visible. The annual publication of progress was required and an annual inspection was to be carried out by Her Majesty's Inspectorate of Constabulary (HMIC) as required by the Macpherson report[23]:

In addition, targets and monitoring were used to influence and persuade black and minority ethnics to consider a career in the police service which was seen to be doing something for the recruitment of ethnic minorities. The annual progress report made by forces in their local area was also used to influence locals into considering the police service and also hope to change their view of the police. "[…] it is inevitable that the black and Asian communities will use this very visible measure to gauge the seriousness of the police intention."[24]

On the other hand, it was recognised that targets put pressure on some police forces in certain areas where these forces found it difficult to recruit minority ethnics to meet government targets. As a result, forces were tempted to recruit ethnic minorities using illegal practices, such as positive discrimination, just to hit targets. In 2006 for instance, two forces, the Gloucestershire Police and the Avon and Somerset Police, obsessed with reaching targets, adopted a kind of 'deselection policy' and rejected white applicants[25]. Though they used positive discrimination to recruit ethnic minorities, their intention could be purely founded on the promotion of diversity within their workforce. However, they were not allowed to do so as positive discrimination, considered as 'reverse discrimination', is illegal. Candidates whose applications were turned down started to think they were being discriminated against because they were white. The question of positive discrimination in the UK was raised following these cases and the confusion between positive action, used by police service to promote equality of opportunity and diversity within the workforce, which is lawful under the Race Relations Act 1976[26], and positive discrimination.

Positive action was a Home Office initiative to enable minority groups to compete for jobs on an equal basis with the majority groups, for instance, by offering special training to the minority groups who are under-represented in the workforce of an institution or by providing additional courses for educational tests[27]. It was not intended to give privileges to minority ethnics but to promote racial justice. Unfortunately, it was too often misunderstood as positive discrimination, also known as 'reverse discrimination' which consists of promoting one group over another group of people.

> [...] there are two people one is an Olympic athlete and has trained for years and years and is ready for the race. The other person has been kept in a prison cell for five years and has been fed on bread and water you put both on the starting line and fire the gun. Who is going to win? If you took this person 'hang on, we are going to put you on a diet plan, we are going to feed you properly, you do some exercises'. Now he can compete in the race

on an equal basis. Now you have the race and may
the best person win. That bit to prepare you for the
race is Positive Action [...]. Positive Discrimination
would be 'oh you Olympic athlete, you wait here
while he starts off'. (*Interview*)

Thames Valley Police say they do not select ethnic
minorities based on race but adopt positive attitudes
towards recruitment. Nevertheless, positive action
was frowned upon within the force. Indeed there was
a growing perception that minority officers were given
preferential treatment and arguments about the reduction
in the standards of the quality of officers.

People say 'Oh he only got promoted because he
is black and black people aren't as good as white
people'. Once the standard of recruits starts to
erode then it becomes a self-fulfilling prophecy
because then people say 'look they let him in but
he is not as good as we are'. If we look at some
of the standards that we are getting in now, I am
concerned that the standards have already started
to be eroded. (*Interview*)

We speak to people who are waiting to join the
police. White people have to wait for a year and
black people have to wait for a month. It already
creates a tension as they would meet each other
at training and they would know they had to wait
longer. That's when they would ask: 'why he had
to wait only a month and I waited for a year?' It
is really divisive only to meet short term targets.
(*Interview*)

Conversely, black and minority groups probably
did not want to be made special, just because they were

black, and would prefer to be recognised and valued for their potential and personal achievement. But, negative perceptions could turn the public and other officers against minority officers and lead to underestimating their potential. "[…] any element of positive discrimination would stigmatise black and Asian recruits as second class police officers."[28]

> If you can get into the police just because you are black and get promoted so where is the achievement in that? [...] Whenever an ethnic minority gets promoted there will be some people who say 'he only got promoted because he is black'. And I know some people must say that about me I suspect. I'd like to think that I have got a good reputation within Thames Valley and people who know me think that actually 'he got promoted because he is good'. But when you are an ethnic minority that is always said behind your back I think. (*Interview*)

Despite the targets, according to recent statistics, in 2002-2003[29], only 9.8 per cent of officers in the Metropolitan police were from minority backgrounds. Though the percentage of minority ethnics was twice as high as in 1999, it seemed that the Metropolitan Police had difficulties in recruiting candidates. In 2005, there were 2.5 per cent of minority officers for a minority population of 5.35 per cent. In 2006-2007 the force had only 3.76 per cent of ethnic minority officers for a minority population of about 6 per cent.

Four main reasons for the lack of potential minority applicants have been found. Firstly, the lack of role models in the force is a barrier to entry for black and minority ethnics. A vicious circle exists, whereby people do not apply unless they see a more diversity in the force but it will never

be diverse unless people apply. In addition, many ethnic
minority officers are leaving during the first two years of their
probationary period, or early in their career if they do not get
promoted. The reasons given are paradoxical.

> We find that ethnic minorities still feature more
> in what we call a regulation 15 procedures which
> is like performance issues which is during their
> probation period. Ethnic minority officers are
> always on the regulation procedures. Sometimes
> people say the reason there are regulation proce-
> dures is because white managers need to be seen
> to be properly managing them. (*Interview*)

Thames Valley Police have a whole retention
strategy in order to help keep police officers in the force
and recognised that using positive discrimination to
increase the numbers was pointless.

> [...] yes we can get as many people in the front
> door as possible but if they are all going out the
> back door within two years what is the point? We
> need to keep them within the organization. [...] the
> more important is not about numbers but where
> they sit within the organization. (*Interview*)

Indeed, the lack of role models particularly in the
senior ranks may explain why minority members, who
wish to move up the ranks and gain promotion, are reluc-
tant to apply. There were no minority officers above the
rank of Chief Superintendent[30].

Secondly, the increasingly diverse ethnic population of
the Thames Valley area makes it difficult for the service to be
reflective of its communities. In Slough, significant numbers
of Polish, Romanians, and Bulgarians settled following the
entry of their countries into the European Union. Simply

employing black and Asian people would not help Thames Valley Police to deal with the Polish community, and would not be reflective of the community. Yet, according to the criteria for entry into the Thames Valley Police Force, Polish people cannot apply to become police officers as they need to have lived in the UK for at least three years.

Finally, the biggest barrier for ethnic minorities was the perception that the police were institutionally racist, white male dominated, sexist. The poor reputation of the police created strong feeling and resentment among the minority communities. According to a senior officer interviewed in 2007, although the police had done more than any other public sector, it was still considered to be the worst on the issue of racism. Their reputation impacted on recruitment which in turn dragged down the image of the service. A white, male dominated colonial culture still appeared to cling to the police force. Nevertheless, 'customer' surveys began to show that positive attitudes were beginning to emerge by 2004 both among white and minority ethnic groups[31].

1. This study references issues found in the UK. What differences do you think US police forces would face in trying to implement the same policies?

2. How do you think using similar hiring and training practices with US police forces would alter the public's perception of police? Do you think the number of accusations of overuse of force would be reduced? Why or why not?

CHAPTER 2

WHAT THE GOVERNMENT AND POLITICIANS SAY

With so much attention on police actions due to activists and the Black Lives Matter movement, both politicians and government research are appearing much more frequently in the public eye with information on how police officers operate. More and more police forces are publishing the results of their research online so that officers in other locales— as well as citizens—can view how police forces are approaching areas of high crime.

The US Commission on Civil Rights is also paying close attention to the issue as noted in their publication "Revisiting *Who Is Guarding the Guardians*," which analyzes the agencies that are overseeing policing in the United States. And the Federal Bureau of Investigation (FBI) is looking into internal issues as demonstrated in Jay Fortenbery's "Improving Motivation and

Productivity of Police Officers," which examines factors that contribute to mental and physical health concerns officers face working in positions where their safety is at risk as part of their daily duties.

All of these governmental inquiries are concerned with increasing the efficiency of police tactics while minimizing any negative outcomes that can arise from ineffective policing. As such, the solutions proposed in these research papers can help make policing safer both for police officers and the communities they serve.

"REVISITING *WHO IS GUARDING THE GUARDIANS?*: A REPORT ON POLICE PRACTICES AND CIVIL RIGHTS IN AMERICA" FROM THE US COMMISSION ON CIVIL RIGHTS, NOVEMBER 2000

EXECUTIVE SUMMARY

For almost 20 years, the U.S. Commission on Civil Rights has been at the forefront of the police practices debate. Through its seminal report titled *Who Is Guarding the Guardians?* and numerous subsequent reports, the Commission has made important recommendations to improve the quality of police protection while ensuring the protection of civil rights for all Americans. The Commission has consistently endeavored to underscore these connected goals.

Law enforcement work is undeniably difficult. Officers must constantly be aware of the pressures to reduce crime and make arrests, while balancing concerns about officer safety and the constant stress of making split-second decisions that could mean the difference between life or death. The Commission applauds the efforts of many law enforcement agencies to improve themselves by increasing diversity among the ranks of officers, developing new training methods on the use of force, and bolstering their internal affairs divisions. Many police departments have also worked to strengthen their relationships with communities of color and have updated their policies in order to adequately respond to the needs of an ever-changing constituency. Some police departments have drastically reduced crime and fundamentally changed the communities in which they serve. Indeed, the Commission found that cities like New York City and Los Angeles, for example, have made great strides in lowering crime rates. These departments have not developed into "world-class" forces, however, due to lingering concerns over the number and types of police misconduct charges they must address.

Regrettably, their crime reduction achievements often have come at a significant cost to the vulnerable communities in greatest need of police protection. Reports of alleged police brutality, harassment, and misconduct continue to spread throughout the country. People of color, women, and the poor are groups of Americans that seem to bear the brunt of the abuse, which compounds the other injustices that they may suffer as a result of discrimination against their racial, ethnic, gender, or economic status. In their eagerness to achieve important goals such as lowering crime, some police officers overstep their authority, trample on individuals' civil rights, and may cause entire communities to fear the same people they hired and trusted to protect them.

Based on the Commission's research, the problem of police misconduct has affected every facet of police culture and policies. Perpetrators can come from any race, ethnicity, or gender, but all police officers are essentially trained by the same law enforcement methods that fail to adequately address cultural diversity and civil rights. Moreover, although law enforcement agencies may significantly reduce crime and the number of police shootings, these improvements come at a terrible price. Incidents of police officers committing crimes, engaging in racial profiling, and harassing individuals continue to make the headlines.

The Commission has a long history of examining the police in their administration of justice and has made numerous recommendations to improve law enforcement as a whole. Many of the Commission's recommendations have been implemented and have positively affected those communities. Despite this fact, reports of abuse and misconduct seem to be incessant, and they typically prompt a complex series of responses: community leaders cry out for change; law enforcement agencies assert that they are doing their job; federal investigators evaluate rogue police officers and entire departments; politicians debate about policies that purport to be tough on crime, yet strong on civil rights. What emerges from these opposing accounts is the need for a reasoned, systematic approach to honestly and sufficiently address police misconduct, once and for all.

By supplementing *Guardians* and its other related reports, the Commission hopes that this publication will move the apparent conflict between law enforcement and civil rights objectives toward a meaningful resolution. Through its findings and recommendations, the Commission presents a comprehensive set of guidelines and objectives to remedy police misconduct, which law enforcement agencies, both federal and state, should fully implement.

Some of the Commission's key findings and recommendations have been previously made in other reports. For example, the Commission reiterates the need to increase diversity in all law enforcement agencies—from the officer patrolling the street to the precinct captain. There is also a continuing need to implement successful models of community policing and to improve police officer training so that it will encompass cultural sensitivity issues and the proper use of force.

In addition, the Commission makes findings and recommendations on the issue of racial profiling that need to be given the highest priority in order to confront this pressing contemporary problem. It has been established that racial profiling exists in many areas of law enforcement. However, profound differences exist between the perceptions of the police and the public, particularly with regard to people of color. People of color and other civilians often conclude that law enforcement officers disproportionately target their communities because of misperceptions about their racial and ethnic backgrounds, rather than crime patterns or citizen complaints. In contrast, many law enforcement officers view race and ethnicity as appropriate elements of proper police investigations. Despite efforts to monitor racial profiling, some police officers and officials resist collecting statistics on alleged suspects' race or ethnicity. It is clear that modified policing techniques, based on facts rather than myths about communities of color, would begin to remedy many of the current problems surrounding this issue. The collection of racial profiling data is needed to examine the extent of its use, to enact legislation to prosecute those who utilize it, and to realize the total elimination of this practice in law enforcement.

RECRUITMENT, SELECTION, PROMOTION, AND RETENTION

Law enforcement personnel generally do not reflect the communities they serve. There continues to be a serious underutilization of people of color and women, as well as bilingual officers. Although police forces have tried to implement affirmative action policies, they have been unable to accomplish or sustain diversity. Several reasons account for this problem. Recruitment efforts do not specifically target women and people of color. Despite attempts to attract members of these groups, many people of color and women continue to have negative perceptions of law enforcement.

Within law enforcement agencies, claims of sexual and racial harassment, disparity in pay, and low job satisfaction make police careers unattractive. Additionally, the selection process for police officers often contains biases that, in effect, eliminate candidates of color and noncitizen permanent residents. The Commission recommends, among other things, that law enforcement agencies:

- Develop creative strategies to increase diversity at all levels.
- Improve public perception of the police to attract more applicants.
- Encourage recruits to have college degrees.
- Eliminate biases in the selection system.
- Revise recruitment and selection methods.

The Commission finds that the promotion and reward systems of many law enforcement agencies are seriously flawed. The emphasis on certain questionable crime reduction strategies may negatively affect civil rights by encouraging officers to engage in unlawful practices in the hopes of gaining a promotion. Indeed, racial profiling may be encouraged by this reward system because communities of color are frequently targeted as "high-crime areas." To remedy this situation, law enforcement agencies should:

- Re-evaluate their retention and promotion processes, recognizing that a system of rewards that promotes crime prevention over the protection of civil rights should be replaced with one that incorporates and reinforces the two concerns.
- Seek ways to improve the promotion rate for officers of color.

TRAINING

Good basic training on diversity issues, especially at the earliest stages of law enforcement careers, would significantly improve the overall effectiveness of officers. In contrast, inadequate training usually reveals itself during the most precarious circumstances: when officers are responding to a volatile crime scene or in the process of making an arrest, and are called upon to make instantaneous, life-altering decisions.

- Effective training must incorporate contemporary issues such as cultural sensitivity, use of force, racial profiling, and community policing into basic crime prevention methods.

- Members of the community should be involved in the training process, so that divergent views and perspectives might be represented.
- Consent decrees with the federal government may also be used to force recalcitrant police departments to comply with federal mandates to improve their training practices.

INTERNAL REGULATION OF LAW ENFORCEMENT AGENCIES

Law enforcement agencies should police themselves primarily because they possess the tools to internally change policies and practices. The Commission finds problems, however, with the internal regulation of the use of deadly force, racial profiling, as well as misconduct investigations and dispositions.

Presumably, all police departments seek to reduce the unnecessary use of deadly force. But different jurisdictions have varying interpretations of the legitimate use of deadly force and the legal standards of reasonable behavior. Civilian deaths caused by police error continue to mount, and it is increasingly evident that officers need clear guidance from their chiefs of police and immediate supervisors on the use of excessive force, as well as internal misconduct policies and disciplinary procedures related to that behavior.

- Police officials should construct a uniform policy on the use of deadly force.
- Intensive training should be provided on a continuing basis to guide officers' discretion.

Internal affairs divisions, charged with investigating allegations of police misconduct and resolving complaints, increasingly lose credibility and effectiveness when they are accused of unequally disciplining the same types of offenses, taking too long to investigate complaints, being unable to break through the code of silence among police officers, failing to keep the public apprised of complaint dispositions, and lacking computerized data systems to track needed information on misconduct incidents.

- Police administrators and IAD officials should routinely examine their disciplinary procedures in order to improve the overall effectiveness of internal affairs divisions.

EXTERNAL CONTROLS

City officials continue to hold the most influence over how external review procedures are conducted. They guide the overall attitude of their officers regarding police misconduct issues.

- Officials at every level of city government should make a concerted effort to eliminate all forms of police misconduct.
- Complete cooperation among government entities and police representatives is necessary to ensure the success of any policy or program designed to address police misconduct.
- Officials should encourage the development of external oversight devices such as civilian review boards, independent auditors, and solicitors general.
- The use of federal monitors to oversee police misconduct issues should be enhanced, especially in

light of the federal civil rights statutes that are in place to address these issues.

- Local law enforcement agencies should be encouraged to cooperate with the efforts of federal monitors.

State prosecution of police misconduct cases is not effective primarily because district or county attorneys rely heavily upon the support and cooperation of police departments.

- The appointment of an independent or special prosecutor assigned solely to police misconduct cases would increase the frequency and quality of those investigations and prosecutions.

Civilian review boards continue to play an important role in the external oversight of police misconduct; however, most boards have little or no investigative or disciplinary powers.

- Subpoena power must be granted to all civilian review boards.
- Civilian review boards should be endowed with disciplinary authority over investigations of police abuse incidents.

REMEDIES AND LEGAL DEVELOPMENTS

The passage of the Violent Crime Control and Law Enforcement Act, which authorizes the Attorney General to bring civil actions against state and local law enforcement agencies that have engaged in a pattern or practice of constitutional rights violations, has been an important development since the publication of *Guardians*. However, the Justice Department has not been adequately funded to realize the full authority provided under the act. Moreover, the act fails to provide for a private right of action by individuals injured by police misconduct.

- Resources must be allocated to fund federal investigations into systemic police misconduct.
- Individuals should be afforded legal standing to sue for equitable and injunctive relief against police departments engaging in misconduct.

Criminal remedies should be pursued in every police misconduct case when there is sufficient evidence to support the charges. Through vigorous criminal prosecution of accused police officers, the federal government can work to remedy the problem of police misconduct. Aggressive federal government tactics could also have a profound effect on the deterrence of further police abuses. But federal prosecution of police officers has been impeded by the provision of 18 U.S.C. § 242, which requires that an allegation of official misconduct be supported by evidence showing that the accused officer acted with a "specific intent" to violate the person's civil rights. In light of the hindrance that this restrictive standard imposes on federal prosecutions,

- Congress should amend § 242 to remove the "specific intent" requirement.
- Federal racketeering laws may serve as alternative methods to pursue criminal charges against offending officers.
- The Justice Department should be properly funded to collect statistics regarding racial profiling.

- The Traffic Stops Statistics Study Act of 1999 should be enacted to further the efforts of that data collection.

CONCLUSION

Police misconduct has a deleterious effect on virtually every aspect of our society. Most importantly, police brutality tears violently at the fabric of our nation, leaving in its aftermath a distrustful and divided community. To improve the effectiveness of our police departments and to decrease tensions between the police and the public, we must find innovative methods to combat police misconduct in all its destructive forms. The Commission hopes that through the collective efforts of the police, the public, and our government, we will someday experience a strengthened bond and a mutual respect between the police and the communities they serve.

1. One of the things the US Commission on Civil Rights mentions as a key factor in issues with police is that "law enforcement personnel generally do not reflect the communities they serve." What do you think the commission means by this and why do you think that might be important?

2. The commission references the "specific intent" clause of a law that governs police misconduct. What do you think this phrase means and why would the commission like it to be removed?

"IMPROVING MOTIVATION AND PRODUCTIVITY OF POLICE OFFICERS," BY JAY FORTENBERY, FROM THE *FBI LAW ENFORCEMENT BULLETIN*, AUGUST 4, 2015

Motivating police personnel can be complicated. Supervisors must work hard to ensure officers perform their duties efficiently and effectively. Many factors can negatively affect productivity and cause officers to become complacent, doing the bare minimum necessary. The difficult nature of crime fighting can cause officers to become cynical toward the population as a whole and develop an "us-versus-them" view.[1] A negative attitude in police work can lead to feelings of inconsequentiality toward law enforcement goals and either slow or stop internal motivation.

Officers who begin their careers with an attitude of "saving the world" can become jaded toward that goal after years of witnessing the worst in people. Constantly observing the aftermath of violent crimes, like robbery, rape, murder, and assault, eventually can take its toll on even the most dedicated officer. Administrators must look for ways to offset this constant bombardment of negativity while reinforcing the positive aspects of society and the benefits provided by quality law enforcement practices.

Considerable research exists addressing motivation that can help administrators facilitate increased productivity, and some results may seem surprising. Extrinsic rewards, like pay raises and educational and longevity pay, often are considered effective motivators. Although pay in the public sector normally is much lower than in private companies, people who become police officers usually are interested in more than a high salary.[2] Intrinsic rewards, such as providing a safe community and reducing crime, can motivate police officers more than pay raises or promotions. Strategies that include internal shifts in assignments that break the monotony of crime fighting in tough neighborhoods also can provide relief for officers on the verge of burnout. Further, rotating officers in and out of high-crime neighborhoods and alternating with patrols in more affluent areas can result in a positive change in attitude.[3]

Generating increased productivity and stimulating individual motivation are constant processes that leaders in any career field always can improve. The profession of law enforcement is no different from others that require ambitious and productive employees to serve effectively, but some aspects of motivation are unique to the professional police officer.

FACTORS

BASIC NEEDS

One of the most commonly cited theories of motivation is that of Abraham Maslow.[4] According to Maslow people are motivated based on a hierarchy of needs. At the bottom of this list are basic physiological essentials, such as food, water, and shelter. After obtaining these necessities, people look for safety, security, and a sense of belonging. Individuals then seek out praise and recognition for a job well-done that is related to a quest for improved self-esteem. This is followed by a desire for self-actualization or the potential to grow professionally.[5]

A prominent feature of this theory is the need for praise and recognition under the self-esteem model.

When properly used by management, praise can be an effective motivator of police personnel. Mark Twain once commented that he could live for 2 months on a compliment alone.[6] Managers who strive to inspire personnel can adopt this adage and use it as an example of motivational philosophy.

STRESS

Conversely, stress can serve as a demotivator if not properly addressed and understood. Law enforcement is broadly considered one of the most stressful occupations and often is associated with high rates of alcoholism, suicide, emotional health problems, and divorce.[7] All of these factors can negatively affect officers' motivation and productivity.

Organizations must strive to recognize and reduce stress associated with the profession to maximize job performance, motivation, and productivity.[8] Although the inherent dangers (e.g., apprehending suspects and facing assaults) of the law enforcement profession create a certain amount of stress, leaders can implement organizational changes that affect supervisory style, field training programs, critical incident counseling, shift work, and job assignments. These internal factors have been rated highly among police officers as major causes of stress. Some officers have reported that the job itself is not as stressful as a call to the supervisor's office.[9]

Several consequences of police stress include cynicism, absenteeism, early retirement, emotional detachment from other aspects of daily life, reduced efficiency, increased complaints, and rises in health problems. In a recent survey, nearly 100 percent of respondents agreed that giving recognition can positively impact morale.[10]

PRAISE AND RECOGNITION

In studies dating back to the 1940s, recognition has out-ranked salary as a strong motivator when pay rates already competitive. Money is an extrinsic motivator, while praise and recognition are intrinsic motivators. Effective leaders must stress the importance of such intrinsic motivators as achievement, recognition, fulfillment, responsibility, advancement, and growth.[11]

SELF-MOTIVATION

Although often considered a responsibility of management, a certain level of motivation must come from within the individual. In a 2003 study on the effects of self-motivation, the actions of police gang unit members in Gothenburg, Sweden were observed. The researcher identified several ways officers can reduce burnout and increase motivation to survive a long career in law enforcement. The intense stress of working constantly in tough, crime-ridden neighborhoods caused officers to desire transfers and redeploy to "nicer" areas as a way to avoid becoming too cynical.[12]

Police officers also can seek different specialized jobs within the organization to help self-motivate and reduce individual stagnation. Large departments often have greater opportunities for internal transfers. Many officers in this study served for several years in the patrol division, then later applied for deployments as investigators, school resource officers, crime prevention officers, or specialized response-team members.[13] These jobs all require different training and varied core job responsibilities that can reinvigorate an officer's professional drive.

Because a substantial part of motivation remains with the officers themselves, the level and need for self-inspiration increases as officers rise in rank to supervisory roles. [14] An important part of a supervisor's function is to lead by example and, above all, have a positive attitude. Self-motivation is a prime ingredient in that formula. According to the U.S. Marine Corps officers' training statement, "Officers have to…self-motivate to keep themselves inspired and focused on the mission. This is the reason they don't sing cadences."[15] If leaders do not motivate themselves, who will do so? And, how can unmotivated leaders expect exceptional performance from subordinates?

Another way persons can increase their own motivation is by examining their strengths and what makes them truly happy and then looking at their weaknesses with a degree of self-examination.[16] For instance, someone could compile a journal with photographs of family members and special events that are inspiring and motivational. By reviewing and adding to the journal regularly, it can serve as a powerful motivator and a reminder for individual inspiration.

ATTITUDE

Research data confirmed that officers' individual attitudes can influence their level of productivity and motivation. In one study officers who perceived traffic enforcement as a personal priority engaged in more enforcement efforts and subsequently issued more citations.[17] They also were influenced by the ideal that management rewarded officers who issued more traffic tickets, and those who agreed with this perception followed suit.

The positive attitudes of the officers' supervisors also resulted in an increase of the number of citations issued. Personnel working for supervisors who perceived traffic problems as a personal priority or under superiors who issued more tickets themselves were more likely to issue additional citations.

HEALTH AND FITNESS

The health and physical fitness of officers also can affect their motivation. Many employers have seen increased absenteeism as a result of employees' health issues.[18] Absent workers strain resources, reduce productivity, and increase costs. In police field units, manpower must be maintained at a minimum level, and illness or injury can cause serious cost overruns in overtime and sick-leave reimbursements. Health insurance costs are steadily rising, and employers pay an average of $13,000 per year, per employee to provide coverage.[19]

Many organizations are moving toward proactive strategies for improving employees' health and fitness to decrease the cost of health coverage. In law enforcement organizations, physical fitness is essential and can impede officer performance if not maintained. Most job descriptions for police officers include lifting, running, jumping, and using force to apprehend and detain criminal suspects. The unique work demands and related stress levels require that those in law enforcement establish lifelong wellness habits.[20]

DISCUSSION

Productivity and motivation are important in any organization. In police agencies, officers have a lot of freedom and discretion and often are unsupervised for many hours of the workday. The individual level of commitment and desire to serve the noble and ethical cause help guide officers' productivity and motivation on the job.[21]

Many variables can influence officers' levels of motivation, including supervisors' attitudes, job environment, and personal factors. Individuals experiencing family problems, health concerns, financial issues, or negative social experiences can exhibit significant declines in productivity and motivation. Job security often can help officers with personal problems as much as a stable personal life can assist them with a difficult work environment.[22] Administrators and direct supervisors seeking to improve work performance should understand this basic psychological process.

The community holds police to a high level of public trust while expecting them to prevent crime, maintain order, and provide an equal and unbiased application of law enforcement. To be an equal opportunity enforcement officer, the individual must be motivated to do the job and held accountable to the highest standards at all times. Fellow officers depend on each other for physical backup, emotional support, and technical guidance.[23] Lack of motivation can be contagious and cause problems for management if not recognized and treated early.

Agencies must have early warning systems in place to recognize symptoms and identify officers experiencing a decline in productivity or a lack of motivation.[24] Computer software programs can recognize possible early warning signs, such as decline in performance, suspicious sick leave patterns, unreasonable uses of force, and increased complaints. Such issues can indicate personal problems that result in a lack of motivation and productivity.

Several theories of motivation exist that supervisors could consider, including Maslow's Hierarchy of Needs, Herzberg's Motivation-Hygiene Theory, and McGregor's X and Y.[25] Administrators can learn many positive, as well as negative, points from these theories, but they all have one thing in common—the idea that supervisors must know their people.[26] To effectively manage motivation and productivity, leaders must possess the human skills needed to work with employees and have the empathy to understand their issues.[27] This idea also means that supervisors must work as a team with officers and build a cooperative effort for the common goal of the agency. By working closely with and understanding officers, effective leaders can identify problems earlier and create effective solutions to deal with those issues.

Physical fitness holds importance when discussing individual motivation and performance. Of course the first step of being productive in an organization is actually coming to work. Officers who participate in regular exercise programs less likely will develop health-related problems that keep them away from the job and negatively affect their work performance.[28] A police officer's job involves interacting with the public, entering and exiting police cars, walking up steps, apprehending suspects, and performing other physical activities dependent on a high level of physical fitness. Law enforcement leaders must take a hard look at agency physical training standards and long-term health programs to help ensure the highest levels of efficiency and effectiveness.[29]

Much of a patrol officer's day is sedentary, often involving seemingly mundane duties, like operating radar from within cars or conducting routine patrol. But, such activities can be interrupted when officers receive calls to apprehend suspects or handle volatile situations. The dramatic increase in heart rate and adrenaline can strain vital organs and muscles not conditioned for this type of response.[30]

Related to health, fitness, and productivity, actual costs are significantly more than once thought. The average employer has $3.00 worth of health-related productivity costs for every $1.00 spent on actual medical expenses.[31] This information is important for administrators and reinforces the reality that healthy employees bode well for business.

The profession of criminal justice is similar to others where the productivity of employees is vital to the bottom line. Whether a business involves farming, sales, construction, teaching, or public safety, evidence indicates that the motivation of the person doing the job is directly proportionate to the level of productivity in that industry.[32] In a criminal justice organization, individual health is important for improving attendance and productivity and related to the safety of the officer and the public. Most law enforcement personnel agree that appropriate physical fitness ensures safe and effective completion of essential job functions.[33]

CONCLUSION

Administrators and managers in law enforcement agencies must remain cognizant of the many factors that can influence individual motivation and productivity of police officers. The nature of the job can result in officer burnout, followed by a decrease in the motivation to perform. Recruits starting out in law enforcement with a strong desire to change the world and who possess a great ethical desire to serve the noble cause easily can be swayed toward mediocrity by the contagiousness of other jaded officers.[34] Although some officers who realize a decline in motivation can self-motivate by seeking out interdepartmental transfers or changes in duty assignments, many police agencies do not have such opportunities. In these smaller organizations, supervisors must work harder to discover other ways to improve an officer's performance.

The intrinsic factors of praise and recognition for a job well-done can help improve officers' attitudes and increase their desire for doing the job. As pointed out in Maslow's Hierarchy of Needs, the need for self-esteem is part of the makeup of all individuals. However, supervisors must rely on this sparingly and in coordination with other methods to avoid crossing the boundary of diminishing returns. Too much emphasis on compliments and recognition easily can ruin officer's effectiveness; therefore, they must be distributed with reason and common sense.

"Administrators also should recognize the stress associated with police work and strive to create a healthy organizational environment where officers are not subjected to harsh leadership. Police officers have sufficient worries while carrying out their responsibilities without the additional stress of managerial problems. [35] When officers perceive interacting with supervisors as causing more stress than dealing with criminals, a fair self-evaluation of management practices clearly is in order.

Management also must set the example for motivation. A positive attitude on the part of a supervisor can directly impact the motivation and productivity of subordinate officers.[36] This makes sense and follows the old saying of "lead by example," a useful adage for all leaders to follow."

Finally, the health and physical wellness of the officer is so important and universally recognized that completion of a physical fitness test is mandated in most recruit training programs.[37] Evidence reveals that the level of vitality and health of employees has an effect on the bottom line of achieving the goals of any organization, and the benefits of physical fitness can directly improve an individual's stress level.[38] Administrators who realize the importance of health and fitness can implement sound strategies and strive to improve the level of well-being within their organizations.

Enhancing the motivation and productivity of police officers is a difficult, yet achievable, objective. When administrators, supervisors, and officers are educated about the many ways this can be achieved, they consistently can work together for the common goal.

1. This article references many factors that can contribute to poor police performance. What would you do to combat the issues cited here? If you were put in charge of a police department, what would you implement to prevent all the issues cited here and why?

CHAPTER 3

WHAT THE COURTS SAY

As with all issues facing the United States, police matters and how police deal with the citizens they protect are subject to an ever-changing legal landscape. In this chapter, we'll examine five court decisions—some federal and some at the Supreme Court level—that impact how police interact with suspects, as well as how the courts view these interactions later if issues are brought before them.

The first is a two-part decision: *Fields v. City of Philadelphia and Geraci v. City of Philadelphia*, in which the decision as to how and when the public is allowed to take video of police interactions is analyzed by Shahid Buttar and Sophia Cope.

The second is *Commonwealth v. Jimmy Warren*, as examined by law scholar Paul Gowder. A landmark case, the decision is the first to acknowledge that black people may not feel safe when confronted by police, and to provide legal protection as a result.

Next are two cases that deal with the use of excessive force. *Constitutional Law Reporter* examines *Plumhoff v. Rickard*, and we'll look at the actual Supreme Court decision in *Kingsley v. Hendrickson*. The first decision is in reference to when the use of deadly force is necessary, and the second—while dealing with what may seem at first glance to be a small issue when it comes to use of force—concerns how force should be viewed by superiors as well as the courts when faced with instances in which excessive force is claimed.

Lastly, Elizabeth E. Joh writes about *Maryland v. King*, which involves how and when DNA can be collected from suspects—even when the suspect has been detained in an unrelated incident.

"COURT'S DECISION ON RECORDING POLICE ERODES FIRST AMENDMENT RIGHTS AND TRANSPARENCY WHILE INVITING VIOLENCE," BY SHAHID BUTTAR AND SOPHIA COPE, FROM THE ELECTRONIC FRONTIER FOUNDATION (EFF), APRIL 6, 2016

A federal district court in Pennsylvania recently issued a terrible joint decision in *Fields v. City of Philadelphia and Geraci v. City of Philadelphia*, holding for the first time that "observing and recording" police activities is not protected by the First Amendment *unless* an observer visibly challenges police conduct in that moment. The right to record police activities, under both the First and Fourth Amendments, is an increasingly vital digital rights issue. If allowed to stand, *Fields* would not only hamstring efforts to improve police accountability, but—given disturbing patterns across the U.S.—could also lead to unnecessary violence.

Criticism of the *Fields* decision emerged quickly, but focused mostly on its artificial distinction between what counts as protected "expression" under the First Amendment and what does not. Unfortunately, that fallacy is merely one among several that pervade the decision.

ARTIFICIAL DISTINCTIONS IN THE LAW

In previous cases emerging from across the country, appellate courts have held that the First Amendment "unambiguously" confers on civilians a right to record police activities, so long as they don't interfere with those activities.

Both the First Circuit (in 2011, in *Glik v. Cunniffe*) and the Seventh Circuit (in 2012, in *ACLU of Illinois v. Alvarez*) have established controlling precedents establishing that rule within their jurisdictions. As a result, residents of Boston and Chicago, for instance, are entitled to observe and record police unless they interfere with them.

In the Third Circuit, however, prior cases failed to resolve whether recording police activity is inherently expressive, or whether instead some other expressive element—such as intending to *share* the photograph to communicate a message—is required to justify First Amendment protection.

In *Kelly v. Borough of Carlisle* (2010), the Third Circuit declined to adopt "a broad right to videotape police" and embraced other cases that "imply that videotaping without an expressive purpose may not be protected." Within this zone of uncertainty, the district court in *Fields* could have agreed with the First and Seventh Circuits and found that "image capture before the decision to transmit the image is, as a matter of law, expressive conduct."

Instead, the court adopted the untenable position that, as a general matter, recording police officers engaged in their public duties is not protected by the First Amendment.

Yet any attempted distinction between clear acts of expression (such as displaying photographs) and their antecedents (taking the photos in the first place) is artificial for First Amendment purposes. In *U.S. v. Stevens* (2010), the Supreme Court struck down a law prohibiting not only the sale and manufacture, but also the creation of films depicting animal cruelty, on the basis that the First Amendment protects both the creation and dissemination of such videos. UCLA law professor Eugene Volokh succinctly illustrates why a distinction between expression and antecedent acts is meaningless:

> Your being able to spend money to express your views is protected even when you don't say anything while writing the check (since your plan is to use the funds to support speech that takes place later).

Even the *Fields* court acknowledged the findings of other courts that "photographing or observing official conduct...is a necessary step in the process of expressing a right to criticize or challenge government behavior." Allowing the suppression of such "a necessary step" inevitably limits subsequent expression. How can an artist or community resident display photos that she was prevented from ever taking?

UNDERMINING TRANSPARENCY

Even if recording police activity were not inherently expressive, it would remain necessary to ensure transparency and police accountability. By denying constitutional protection to observers of police who take care to avoid interfering with officers' activities while recording, the *Fields* decision undermines community oversight. As described by the Cato Institute's Adam Bates:

> The ability of individuals to record police in public *without fear of reprisal* is an essential mechanism for injecting transparency where it is sorely lacking, for holding the government accountable for misconduct, and in many cases for protecting good police officers from misattributed blame. (emphasis added)

The incentives constructed by *Fields* would undermine this "essential mechanism for...transparency," by inviting police officers to either suppress recordings of potential abuse (as they did in both of the cases before the court) or contrive their actions when they are being recorded. As photographer and journalist Jeremy Gray writes:

> If you are required to announce to police that you're recording them...what are the chances that any illegal conduct that you had been observing will continue when you start taking photos?

More fundamentally, as noted by Reggie Shuford at the ACLU of Pennsylvania, "The freedom to monitor the police without fearing arrest or retaliation is one of the ways we distinguish a free society from a police state."

INVITING POLICE DISCRETION, WITH DANGEROUS CONSEQUENCES

An objective, "bright line" rule recognizing First Amendment protection for recording police engaged in their public duties, regardless of the purpose, not only facilitates community oversight, but also facilitates decision-making by both police officers and judges. In contrast, a requirement that photographers demonstrate a hostile purpose in order to secure constitutional protection for recording police invites discretion that is difficult—and dangerous—to apply.

How, exactly, is a police officer supposed to recognize whether someone recording their activities is hostile? Is it reasonable to expect—or even ask—police to give overtly hostile people wider berth than others who calmly observe, as the plaintiffs in these cases tried to do?

By perversely encouraging adversarial relations with police, *Fields* essentially requires civilians and photojournalists to risk police retaliation in order to exercise a constitutional right. Such retaliation often includes physical violence (as Ms. Geraci endured while being denied her right to record), arbitrary arrest, and contrived charges such as "assault on a police officer."

A further tension emerges in light of prior cases sharply distinguishing *observing and recording* police activities (recognized as constitutionally protected acts) from acts *interfering* with police activities, which remain within the state's authority to legitimately prohibit. In order for a police accountability activist like Ms. Geraci to gain constitutional protection under *Fields*, she would have to risk prosecution under the rule in *Alvarez*.

Moreover, judging from their behavior in the instances before the court, the police in these cases *did* think the plaintiffs were hostile, leading them to detain Fields and seize his phone, and to "attack" Geraci and restrain her from taking photos. At least in Geraci's case, they were right: she trained with Cop Watch Berkeley and was visibly associated with organizers of a protest that she was observing specifically to record any possible police misconduct.

The district court's failure to correctly apply its own subjective standard to the facts of *Fields* and *Geraci* reflects yet another reason why *Fields* was incorrectly decided: it invents a rule that is simply inadministrable, impossible to apply consistently across differing facts.

UNDERMINING COMMUNITIES VULNERABLE TO POLICE VIOLENCE

People who record police rarely do so recreationally. They usually do so because, around the country, evidence has emerged that police apply unnecessary force and even kill innocent people with disturbing frequency. In this context, *Fields* places at risk not only the rights of millions of people, but also their safety.

By limiting constitutional protection for recording police, *Fields* denies vulnerable communities the essential tool that has exposed the public, courts, and Congress to recurring acts of police violence prohibited under the law. *Fields* would not only expose individuals to police retaliation for acts of civic engagement, but also make their communities more vulnerable to systemic patterns of arbitrary police abuses.

The decision's failure to even address this outcome implicit in its reasoning, let alone its various other defects, renders it worthy of prompt reversal. We eagerly await the Third Circuit's ruling in a forthcoming appeal to correct this novel, unprecedented, and ultimately dangerous ruling.

1. The EFF obviously believes this court decision is detrimental to citizen rights. Do you agree? Why or why not?

2. This article claims the court's decision is "inadministrable." What facets do you think are difficult for police and citizens to deal with?

"A SMALL SIGN OF HOPE ON THIS DARK DAY FOR THE MOVEMENT FOR BLACK LIVES," BY PAUL GOWDER, FROM *MEDIUM*, SEPTEMBER 20, 2016

Today we lost two more African-Americans to the police: Terence Crutcher and Keith Lamont Scott. And we know what comes next: the political fighting starts, the protestors get labeled "agitators" and apologists start to spin the usual stories about how they looked armed, or were disobeying police orders, more systemic discrimination gets turned up in more departments.

But **today there is also a bright point** in the perennial battle to teach the police and the political establishment that black lives matter. The **Massachusetts Supreme Judicial Court**—the state's highest court—has come as close as we can expect any high court in the United States to come in the near future to an outright endorsement of the movement for black lives. **The Court outright ruled that it's rational and understandable for black people to** run from the police because, and this is a direct quote, of the "indignity of racial profiling." And unless I'm missing some dissent that hasn't come out yet, the decision is *unanimous.*

"HE FIT THE DESCRIPTION."

Commonwealth v. Jimmy Warren was a case about a black man who was stopped because he "fit the description." He fled from the police, and when they caught him, they also found an unlicensed weapon nearby. They got a conviction for the unlicensed weapon, but he challenged it on appeal on the grounds that they had no grounds to stop him in the first place.

The relevant legal rule is that the police have to have "reasonable suspicion" before they detain someone. But **the Massachusetts high court found that the police did not have reasonable suspicion, and reversed his conviction. Their explanation why is nothing less than an indictment of racist policing**.

First, they called out the classic "fits the description" bullshit. Here's the Court, lightly edited for clarity, to remove internal citations and quotation marks, etc.:

First, and perhaps most important, because the victim had given a very general description of the perpetrator and his accomplices, the police did not know whom they were looking for that evening, except that the suspects were three black males: two black males wearing the ubiquitous and nondescriptive "dark clothing," and one black male wearing a "red hoodie." Lacking any information about facial features, hairstyles, skin tone, height, weight, or other physical characteristics, the victim's description contributed nothing to the officers' ability to distinguish the defendant from any other black male" wearing dark clothes and a "hoodie" in Roxbury. With only this vague description, it was simply not possible for the police reasonably and rationally to target the defendant or any other black male wearing dark clothing as a suspect in the crime.

That's already huge. The Supreme Judicial Court just slapped the police down for claiming that they had the power to do anything based on a "description" that fit half the black men in town. But it just gets better.

"HEY BUDDY, I'D LIKE TO TALK TO YOU."

See, one of the things the police claimed, and the lower court accepted, was that the police had reasonable suspicion to detain him, because when the cop came up to invite Warren to "voluntarily" talk to him, Warren ran away.

This is another classic police move: it turns out the initial conversation isn't really voluntary after all, because exercising your right to not participate in the conversation just gives them an excuse to involuntarily interrogate you. But the Court was having none of that noise. First, it acknowledged that the doctrine as it stands is nonsensical (even as it reluctantly retained it):

First, we perceive a factual irony in the consideration of flight as a factor in the reasonable suspicion calculus. Unless reasonable suspicion for a threshold inquiry already exists, our law guards a person's freedom to speak or not to speak to a police officer. A person also may choose to walk away, avoiding altogether any contact with police. Yet, because flight is viewed as inculpatory, we have endorsed it as a factor in the reasonable suspicion analysis.

But then it dropped the bomb.

JUDICIAL ANTI-RACIST MIC DROP:

Second, as set out by one of the dissenting Justices in the Appeals court opinion, where the suspect is a black male stopped by the police on the streets of Boston, the analysis of flight as a factor in the reasonable suspicion calculus cannot be divorced from the findings in a recent Boston Police Department (department) report documenting a pattern of racial profiling of black males in the city of Boston. According to the study, based on FIO [Field Interrogation and Observation] data collected by the department, black men in the city of Boston were more likely to be targeted for police-civilian encounters such as stops, frisks, searches, observations, and inter-rogations. Black men were also disproportionally targeted for repeat police encounters. We do not eliminate flight as a factor in the reasonable suspicion analysis whenever a black male is the subject of an investigatory stop. However, in such circumstances, flight is not necessarily probative of a suspect's state of mind or consciousness of guilt. Rather, the finding that black males in Boston are disproportionately and repeatedly targeted for FIO encounters suggests a reason for flight totally unrelated to consciousness of guilt. Such an individual, when approached by the police, might just as easily be motivated by the desire to avoid the recurring indignity of being racially profiled as by the desire to hide criminal activity. Given this reality for black males in the city of Boston, a judge should, in appropriate cases, consider the report's findings in weighing flight as a factor in the reasonable suspicion calculus.

Let me translate that for you. **Because of racial profiling, the court refused to allow the police to infer that a black man who ran away from them was guilty of something.**

Ordinarily, the police could say that running away meant he was guilty of something, but because there's so much evidence that the Boston police are flat-out racist, black people have plenty of reason to run from them, reason that has nothing to do with being guilty of anything.

I know it doesn't sound like much behind all the legalese, but this is really huge. A state Supreme Court just officially acknowledged that it's perfectly reasonable for black people to run from the cops, because of systemic police racism. This is a much, much, much needed sign of hope as we see more police killings of black folks piling up.

Black lives matter.

1. In the court case referenced here (*Commonwealth v. Jimmy Warren*), Massachusetts Courts gave black citizens the right to flee police. How might this decision impact policing practices such as "hot spots"?

2. Do you agree with the Court's decision that by claiming a black person running from police is "acting guilty" there is reasonable suspicion of criminal activity? Why or why not?

"*PLUMHOFF V. RICKARD*: WHEN IS POLICE USE OF DEADLY FORCE JUSTIFIED?" BY DONALD SCARINCI, FROM *CONSTITUTIONAL LAW REPORTER*, SEPTEMBER 4, 2014

In *Plumhoff v. Rickard*, the U.S. Supreme Court addressed what type of law enforcement conduct rises to the level of "excessive force in violation of the Constitution. The 2014 decision may play a role in whether the Ferguson, Missouri police officer that shot and killed unarmed teenager Michael Brown is ultimately prosecuted and convicted.

THE FACTS OF THE CASE

Following a traffic stop, Donald Rickard led police officers on a high-speed car chase until he eventually spun out into a parking lot. Although his vehicle was cornered by a patrol car, Rickard continued to press the accelerator. In response, an officer fired three shots into Rickard's car. However, he was able to drive away, narrowly missing an officer in the process. Officers fired 12 more shots as Rickard sped away, striking him and his passenger, both of whom died from their injuries.

Rickard's minor daughter filed a 42 U. S. C. §1983 action, alleging that the officers used excessive force,

violating the 4th and 14th Amendments. The suit specifically alleged that Fourth Amendment did not allow the
officers to use deadly force to terminate the chase, and
that, even if they were permitted to fire their weapons,
they went too far when they fired as many rounds as
they did. The District Court denied the officers' motion
for summary judgment based on qualified immunity after
finding that their conduct violated the Fourth Amendment
and was contrary to clearly established law at the time in
question. The Sixth Circuit Court of Appeals affirmed.

THE LEGAL BACKGROUND

Claims of excessive [force] are governed by the Fourth
Amendment's "reasonableness" standard, per the Court's
decision in *Graham v. Connor*. This standard "requires a
careful balancing of the nature and quality of the intrusion
on the individual's Fourth Amendment interests against the
countervailing governmental interests at stake." Given that
officers are frequently required to make split second decisions, courts are required to analyze this question from the
perspective "of a reasonable officer on the scene, rather
than with the 20/20 vision of hindsight." *Id.*

THE COURT'S DECISION

In a unanimous decision, the justices concluded that the
officers' conduct did not violate the Fourth Amendment.
With regard to the use of deadly force, the court concluded
that the officers actions were reasonable, citing *Scott
v. Harris*, in which the Court held that a "police officer's
attempt to terminate a dangerous high-speed car chase
that threatens the lives of innocent bystanders does not

violate the Fourth Amendment, even when it places the fleeing motorist at risk of serious injury or death."

In this case, the Court noted that "Rickard's outrageously reckless driving—which lasted more than five minutes, exceeded 100 miles per hour, and included the passing of more than two dozen other motorists—posed a grave public safety risk, and the record conclusively disproves that the chase was over when Rickard's car came to a temporary standstill and officers began shooting. Under the circumstances when the shots were fired, all that a reasonable officer could have concluded from Rickard's conduct was that he was intent on resuming his flight, which would again pose a threat to others on the road."

The justices also concluded that the officers did not fire more shots than necessary to end the public safety risk. As explained by the Court, it "stands to reason that, if police officers are justified in firing at a suspect in order to end a severe threat to public safety, the officers need not stop shooting until the threat has ended."

1. Why do you think the court referenced a previous decision in this case using the phrase "of a reasonable officer on the scene, rather than with the 20/20 vision of hindsight."? How do you think that legal precedent affected the outcome of this case?

2. Based on this decision, what do you think the definition of "excessive force" would be? Explain how you came to this conclusion.

EXCERPT FROM *KINGSLEY V. HENDRICKSON ET AL.*, FROM THE SUPREME COURT OF THE UNITED STATES, JUNE 22, 2015

SYLLABUS

While petitioner Kingsley was awaiting trial in county jail, officers forcibly removed him from his cell when he refused to comply with their instructions. Kingsley filed a complaint in Federal District Court claiming, as relevant here, that two of the officers used excessive force against him in violation of the Fourteenth Amendment's Due Process Clause. At the trial's conclusion, the District Court instructed the jury that Kingsley was required to prove, *inter alia*, that the officers "recklessly disregarded [Kingsley's] safety" and "acted with reckless disregard of [his] rights." The jury found in the officers' favor. On appeal, Kingsley argued that the jury instruction did not adhere to the proper standard for judging a pretrial detainee's excessive force claim, namely, objective unreasonableness. The Seventh Circuit disagreed, holding that the law required a subjective inquiry into the officers' state of mind, *i.e.,* whether the officers actually intended to violate, or recklessly disregarded, Kingsley's rights.

Held:

1. Under 42 U. S. C. §1983, a pretrial detainee must show only that the force purposely or knowingly used against him was objectively unreasonable to prevail on an excessive force claim. Pp. 5–13.

(a) This determination must be made from the perspective of a reasonable officer on the scene, including what the officer knew at the time, see

Graham v. *Connor,* 490 U. S. 386, and must account for the "legitimate interests [stemming from the government's] need to manage the facility in which the individual is detained," appropriately deferring to "policies and practices that in th[e] judgment" of jail officials "are needed to preserve internal order and discipline and to maintain institutional security," *Bell* v. *Wolfish,* 441 U. S. 520, 540, 547. Pp. 5–7.

(b) Several considerations lead to this conclusion. An objective standard is consistent with precedent. In *Bell,* for instance, this Court held that a pretrial detainee could prevail on a claim that his due process rights were violated by providing only objective evidence that the challenged governmental action was not rationally related to a legitimate governmental objective or that it was excessive in relation to that purpose. 441 U. S., at 541–543. Cf. *Block* v. *Rutherford,* 468 U. S. 576–586. Experience also suggests that an objective standard is workable. It is consistent with the pattern jury instructions used in several Circuits, and many facilities train officers to interact with detainees as if the officers' conduct is subject to objective reasonableness. Finally, the use of an objective standard adequately protects an officer who acts in good faith, *e.g.,* by acknowledging that judging the reasonableness of the force used from the perspective and with the knowledge of the defendant officer is an appropriate part of the analysis. Pp. 7–10.

(c) None of the cases respondents point to provides significant support for a subjective standard.

Whitley v. *Albers*, 475 U. S. 312, and *Hudson* v.
McMillian, 503 U. S. 1, lack relevance in this context
because they involved claims brought by convicted
prisoners under the Eighth Amendment's Cruel and
Unusual Punishment Clause, not claims brought by
pretrial detainees under the Fourteenth Amendment's
Due Process Clause. And in *County of Sacramento* v.
Lewis, 523 U. S. 833, a statement indicating the need to
show "purpose to cause harm," *id.,* at 854, for due process liability refers not to whether the force intentionally used was excessive, but whether the defendant
intended to commit the acts in question, *id.,* at 854, and
n. 13. Finally, in *Johnson* v. *Glick*, 481 F. 2d 1028 (CA2), a
malicious-and-sadistic-purpose-to-cause-harm factor
was not suggested as a *necessary* condition for liability, but as a factor, among others, that might help show
that the use of force was excessive. Pp. 10–13.

2. Applying the proper standard, the jury instruction
was erroneous. Taken together, the features of that
instruction suggested that the jury should weigh
respondents' subjective reasons for using force
and subjective views about the excessiveness of
that force. Respondents' claim that, irrespective of
this Court's holding, any error in the instruction was
harmless is left to the Seventh Circuit to resolve on
remand. Pp. 13–14.

744 F. 3d 443, vacated and remanded.
Breyer, J., delivered the opinion of the Court, in which
Kennedy, Ginsburg, Sotomayor, and Kagan, JJ., joined.
Scalia, J., filed a dissenting opinion, in which Roberts, C. J.,
and Thomas, J., joined. Alito, J., filed a dissenting opinion.

OPINION

Justice Breyer delivered the opinion of the Court.

In this case, an individual detained in a jail prior to trial brought a claim under Rev. Stat. §1979, 42 U. S. C. §1983, against several jail officers, alleging that they used excessive force against him, in violation of the Fourteenth Amendment's Due Process Clause. The officers concede that they intended to use the force that they used. But the parties disagree about whether the force used was excessive.

The question before us is whether, to prove an excessive force claim, a pretrial detainee must show that the officers were *subjectively* aware that their use of force was unreasonable, or only that the officers' use of that force was *objectively* unreasonable. We conclude that the latter standard is the correct one.

I

A

Some but not all of the facts are undisputed: Michael Kingsley, the petitioner, was arrested on a drug charge and detained in a Wisconsin county jail prior to trial. On the evening of May 20, 2010, an officer performing a cell check noticed a piece of paper covering the light fixture above Kingsley's bed. The officer told Kingsley to remove it; Kingsley refused; subsequently other officers told Kingsley to remove the paper; and each time Kingsley refused. The next morning, the jail administrator, Lieutenant Robert Conroy, ordered Kingsley to remove the paper. Kingsley once again refused. Conroy then told Kingsley that officers would remove the paper and that he would be moved to a receiving cell in the interim.

Shortly thereafter, four officers, including respondents Sergeant Stan Hendrickson and Deputy Sheriff Fritz Degner, approached the cell and ordered Kingsley to stand, back up to the door, and keep his hands behind him. When Kingsley refused to comply, the officers handcuffed him, forcibly removed him from the cell, carried him to a receiving cell, and placed him face down on a bunk with his hands handcuffed behind his back.

The parties' views about what happened next differ. The officers testified that Kingsley resisted their efforts to remove his handcuffs. Kingsley testified that he did not resist. All agree that Sergeant Hendrickson placed his knee in Kingsley's back and Kingsley told him in impolite language to get off. Kingsley testified that Hendrickson and Degner then slammed his head into the concrete bunk—an allegation the officers deny.

The parties agree, however, about what happened next: Hendrickson directed Degner to stun Kingsley with a Taser; Degner applied a Taser to Kingsley's back for approximately five seconds; the officers then left the handcuffed Kingsley alone in the receiving cell; and officers returned to the cell 15 minutes later and removed Kingsley's handcuffs.

B

Based on these and related events, Kingsley filed a §1983 complaint in Federal District Court claiming (among other things) that Hendrickson and Degner used excessive force against him, in violation of the Fourteenth Amendment's Due Process Clause. The officers moved for summary judgment, which the District Court denied, stating that "a reasonable jury could conclude that [the officers] acted with malice and intended to harm [Kingsley] when they used force against him." *Kingsley* v. *Josvai*, No. 10–cv–832–bbc (WD Wis., Nov. 16, 2011), App to Pet. for Cert. 66a–67a. Kingsley's excessive force claim accordingly proceeded to trial. At the conclusion of the trial, the District Court instructed the jury as follows:

"Excessive force means force *applied recklessly* that is unreasonable in light of the facts and circumstances of the time. Thus, to succeed on his claim of excessive use of force, plaintiff must prove each of the following factors by a preponderance of the evidence:

"(1) Defendants used force on plaintiff;

"(2) Defendants' use of force was unreasonable in light of the facts and circumstances at the time;

"(3) Defendants knew that using force presented a risk of harm to plaintiff, but they recklessly disregarded plaintiff's safety by failing to take reasonable measures to minimize the risk of harm to plaintiff; and

"(4) Defendants' conduct caused some harm to plaintiff.

"In deciding whether one or more defendants used 'unreasonable' force against plaintiff, you must consider whether it was unreasonable from the perspective of a reasonable officer facing the same circumstances that defendants faced. You must make this decision based on what defendants knew at the time of the incident, not based on what you know now.

CRITICAL PERSPECTIVES ON EFFECTIVE POLICING AND
POLICE BRUTALITY

"Also, in deciding whether one or more defendants used unreasonable force and acted with *reckless disregard of plaintiff 's rights*, you may consider factors such as:

"• The need to use force;

"• The relationship between the need to use force and the amount of force used;

"• The extent of plaintiff's injury;

"• Whether defendants reasonably believed there was a threat to the safety of staff or prisoners; and

"• Any efforts made by defendants to limit the amount of force used." App. 277–278 (emphasis added).

The jury found in the officers' favor.

On appeal, Kingsley argued that the correct standard for judging a pretrial detainee's excessive force claim is objective unreasonableness. And, the jury instruction, he said, did not hew to that standard. A panel of the Court of Appeals disagreed, with one judge dissenting. The majority held that the law required a "subjective inquiry" into the officer's state of mind. There must be " 'an actual intent to violate [the plaintiff's] rights or reckless disregard for his rights.' " 744 F. 3d 443, 451 (CA7 2014) (quoting *Wilson* v. *Williams*, 83 F. 3d 870, 875 (CA7 1996)). The dissent would have used instructions promulgated by the Committee on Pattern Civil Jury Instructions of the Seventh Circuit, which require a pretrial detainee claiming excessive force to show only that the use of force was objectively unreasonable. 744 F. 3d, at 455 (opinion of Hamilton, J.); see Pattern Civ. Jury Instr. §7.08 (2009). The dissent further stated that the District Court's use of the word "reckless" in the jury instruction added "an unnecessary and confusing element." 744 F. 3d, at 455.

Kingsley filed a petition for certiorari asking us to determine whether the requirements of a §1983 excessive force claim brought by a pretrial detainee must satisfy the subjective standard or only the objective standard. In light of disagreement among the Circuits, we agreed to do so. Compare, *e.g., Murray* v. *Johnson No. 260,* 367 Fed. Appx. 196, 198 (CA2 2010); *Bozeman* v. *Orum,* 422 F. 3d 1265, 1271 (CA11 2005) (*per curiam*), with *Aldini* v. *Johnson,* 609 F. 3d 858, 865–866 (CA6 2010); *Young* v. *Wolfe,* 478 Fed. Appx. 354, 356 (CA9 2012).

II

A

We consider a legally requisite state of mind. In a case like this one, there are, in a sense, two separate state-of-mind questions. The first concerns the defendant's state of mind with respect to his physical acts—*i.e.,* his state of mind with respect to the bringing about of certain physical consequences in the world. The second question concerns the defendant's state of mind with respect to whether his use of force was "excessive." Here, as to the first question, there is no dispute. As to the second, whether to interpret the defendant's physical acts in the world as involving force that was "excessive," there is a dispute. We conclude with respect to that question that the relevant standard is objective not subjective. Thus, the defendant's state of mind is not a matter that a plaintiff is required to prove.

Consider the series of physical events that take place in the world—a series of events that might consist, for example, of the swing of a fist that hits a face, a push that leads to a fall, or the shot of a Taser that leads to the stunning of its recipient. No one here denies, and we must assume, that, as to the series of events that have taken place in the world, the defendant must possess a purposeful, a knowing, or possibly a reckless state of mind. That is because, as we have stated, "liability for *negligently* inflicted harm is categorically beneath the threshold of constitutional due process." *County of Sacramento* v. *Lewis*, 523 U. S. 833, 849 (1998) (emphasis added). See also *Daniels* v. *Williams*, 474 U. S. 327, 331 (1986) ("Historically, this guarantee of due process has been applied to *deliberate* decisions of government officials to deprive a person of life, liberty, or property"). Thus, if an officer's Taser goes off by accident or if an officer unintentionally trips and falls on a detainee, causing him harm, the pretrial detainee cannot prevail on an excessive force claim. But if the use of force is deliberate—*i.e.,* purposeful or knowing—the pretrial detainee's claim may proceed. In the context of a police pursuit of a suspect the Court noted, though without so holding, that recklessness in some cases might suffice as a standard for imposing liability. See *Lewis, supra,* at 849. Whether that standard might suffice for liability in the case of an alleged mistreatment of a pretrial detainee need not be decided here; for the officers do not dispute that they acted purposefully or knowingly with respect to the force they used against Kingsley.

We now consider the question before us here—the defendant's state of mind with respect to the proper *interpretation* of the force (a series of events in the world) that the defendant deliberately (not accidentally or negligently) used. In deciding whether the force deliberately used is, constitutionally speaking, "excessive," should courts use an objective standard only, or instead a subjective standard that takes into account a defendant's state of mind? It is with respect to *this* question that we hold that courts must use an objective standard. In short, we agree with the dissenting appeals court judge, the Seventh Circuit's jury instruction committee, and Kingsley, that a pretrial detainee must show only that the force purposely or knowingly used against him was objectively unreasonable.

A court (judge or jury) cannot apply this standard mechanically. See *Lewis, supra,* at 850. Rather, objective reasonableness turns on the "facts and circumstances of each particular case." *Graham* v. *Connor,* 490 U. S. 386, 396 (1989) . A court must make this determination from the perspective of a reasonable officer on the scene, including what the officer knew at the time, not with the 20/20 vision of hindsight. See *ibid.* A court must also account for the "legitimate interests that stem from [the government's] need to manage the facility in which the individual is detained," appropriately deferring to "policies and practices that in th[e] judgment" of jail officials "are needed to preserve internal order and discipline and to maintain institutional security." *Bell* v. *Wolfish,* 441 U. S. 520, 540, 547 (1979) .

Considerations such as the following may bear on the reasonableness or unreasonableness of the force used: the relationship between the need for the use of force and the amount of force used; the extent of the plaintiff's injury; any effort made by the officer to temper or to limit the amount of force; the severity of the security problem at issue; the threat reasonably perceived by the officer; and whether the plaintiff was actively resisting. See, *e.g., Graham, supra,* at **396**. We do not consider this list to be exclusive. We mention these factors only to illustrate the types of objective circumstances potentially relevant to a determination of excessive force.

B

Several considerations have led us to conclude that the appropriate standard for a pretrial detainee's excessive force claim is solely an objective one. For one thing, it is consistent with our precedent. We have said that "the Due Process Clause protects a pretrial detainee from the use of excessive force that amounts to punishment." *Graham, supra,* at **395**, n. **10**. And in *Bell,* we explained that such "punishment" can consist of actions taken with an "expressed intent to punish." **441** U. S., at **538**. But the *Bell* Court went on to explain that, in the absence of an expressed intent to punish, a pretrial detainee can nevertheless prevail by showing that the actions are not "rationally related to a legitimate nonpunitive governmental purpose" or that the actions "appear excessive in relation to that purpose." *Id.,* at **561**. The *Bell* Court applied this latter objective standard to evaluate a variety of prison conditions, including a prison's practice of double-bunking. In doing so, it did not consider the prison officials' subjective beliefs about the policy. *Id.,* at **541–543**. Rather, the Court examined objective evidence, such as the size of the rooms and available amenities, before concluding that the conditions were reasonably related to the legitimate purpose of holding detainees for trial and did not appear excessive in relation to that purpose. *Ibid.*

WHAT THE COURTS SAY

Bell's focus on "punishment" does not mean that proof of intent (or motive) to punish is required for a pretrial detainee to prevail on a claim that his due process rights were violated. Rather, as *Bell* itself shows (and as our later precedent affirms), a pretrial detainee can prevail by providing only objective evidence that the challenged governmental action is not rationally related to a legitimate governmental objective or that it is excessive in relation to that purpose. Cf. *Block* v. *Rutherford*, 468 U. S. 576–586 (1984) (where there was no suggestion that the purpose of jail policy of denying contact visitation was to punish inmates, the Court need only evaluate whether the policy was "reasonably related to legitimate governmental objectives" and whether it appears excessive in relation to that objective); *Schall* v. *Martin*, 467 U. S. 253–271 (1984) (similar); see also *United States* v. *Salerno*, 481 U. S. 739, 747 (1987) ("[T]he punitive/regulatory distinction *turns on* 'whether an alternative purpose to which [the restriction] may rationally be connected is assignable for it, and whether it appears excessive in relation to the alternative purpose assigned [to it]'" (quoting *Schall, supra*, at 269; emphasis added and some internal quotation marks omitted)). The Court did not suggest in any of these cases, either by its words or its analysis, that its application of *Bell's* objective standard should involve subjective considerations. Our standard is also consistent with our use of an objective "excessive force" standard where officers apply force to a person who, like Kingsley, has been accused but not convicted of a crime, but who, unlike Kingsley, is free on bail. See *Graham, supra*.

For another thing, experience suggests that an objective standard is workable. It is consistent with the pattern jury instructions used in several Circuits. We are also told that many facilities, including the facility at issue here, train officers to interact with all detainees as if the officers' conduct is subject to an objective reasonableness standard. See Brief for Petitioner 26; App. 247–248; Brief for Former Corrections Administrators and Experts as *Amici Curiae* 8–18.

Finally, the use of an objective standard adequately protects an officer who acts in good faith. We recognize that "[r]unning a prison is an inordinately difficult undertaking," *Turner* v. *Safley*, 482 U. S. 78–85 (1987), and that "safety and order at these institutions requires the expertise of correctional officials, who must have substantial discretion to devise reasonable solutions to the problems they face," *Florence* v. *Board of Chosen Freeholders of County of Burlington*, 566 U. S. ___, ___ (2012) (slip op., at 5). Officers facing disturbances "are often forced to make split-second judgments—in circumstances that are tense, uncertain, and rapidly evolving." *Graham*, 490 U. S., at 397. For these reasons, we have stressed that a court must judge the reasonableness of the force used from the perspective and with the knowledge of the defendant officer. We have also explained that a court must take account of the legitimate interests in managing a jail, acknowledging as part of the objective reasonableness analysis that deference to policies and practices needed to maintain order and institutional security is appropriate. See Part II–A, *supra.* And we have limited liability for excessive force to situations in which the use of force was the result of an intentional and knowing act (though we leave open the possibility of including a "reckless" act as well). *Ibid.* Additionally, an officer enjoys qualified immunity and is not liable for excessive force unless he has violated a "clearly established" right, such that "it would [have been] clear to a reasonable officer that his conduct was unlawful in the situation he confronted." *Saucier* v. *Katz*, 533 U. S. 194, 202 (2001) ; see also Brief for United States as *Amicus Curiae* 27–28. It is unlikely (though theoretically possible) that a plaintiff could overcome these hurdles where an officer acted in good faith.

C

Respondents believe that the relevant legal standard should be subjective, *i.e.,* that the plaintiff must prove that the use of force was not "applied in a good-faith effort to maintain or restore discipline" but, rather, was applied "maliciously and sadistically to cause harm." Brief for Respondents 27. And they refer to several cases that they believe support their position. See *id.,* at 26–31 (citing *Whitley* v. *Albers*, 475 U. S. 312 (1986) ; *Hudson* v. *McMillian*, 503 U. S. 1 (1992) ; *Lewis*, 523 U. S. 833; *Johnson* v. *Glick*, 481 F. 2d 1028 (CA2 1973)).

The first two of these cases, however, concern excessive force claims brought by convicted prisoners under the Eighth Amendment's Cruel and Unusual Punishment Clause, not claims brought by pretrial detainees under the Fourteenth Amendment's Due Process Clause. *Whitley*, *supra*, at 320; *Hudson*, *supra*, at 6–7. The language of the two Clauses differs, and the nature of the claims often differs. And, most importantly, pretrial detainees (unlike convicted prisoners) cannot be punished at all, much less "maliciously and sadistically." *Ingraham* v. *Wright*, 430 U. S. 651–672, n. 40 (1977); *Graham, supra*, at 395, n. 10 (1989); see also 4 W. Blackstone, Commentaries *300 ("[I]f the offence be not bailable, or the party cannot find bail, he is to be committed to the county [jail] . . . [b]ut . . . only for safe custody, and not for punishment"). Thus, there is no need here, as there might be in an Eighth Amendment case, to determine when punishment is unconstitutional. *Whitley* and *Hudson* are relevant here only insofar as they address the practical importance of taking into account the legitimate safety-related concerns of those who run jails. And, as explained above, we believe we have done so.

Lewis does not prove respondents' point, either. There, the Court considered a claim that a police officer had violated due process by causing a death during a high-speed automobile chase aimed at apprehending a suspect. We wrote that "[j]ust as a purpose to cause harm is needed for Eighth Amendment liability in a [prison] riot case, so it ought to be needed for due process liability in a pursuit case." 523 U. S., at 854. Respondents contend that this statement shows that the Court embraced a standard for due process claims that requires a showing of subjective intent. Brief for Respondents 30–31. Other portions of the *Lewis* opinion make clear, however, that this statement referred to the defendant's intent to commit the *acts* in question, not to whether the force intentionally used was "excessive." 523 U. S., at 854, and n. 13. As explained above, the parties here do not dispute that respondents' use of force was intentional. See Part II–A, *supra*.

Nor does *Glick* provide respondents with significant support. In that case Judge Friendly, writing for the Second Circuit, considered an excessive force claim brought by a pretrial detainee under the Fourteenth Amendment's Due Process Clause. Judge Friendly pointed out that the "management by a few guards of large numbers of prisoners" in an institution "may require and justify the occasional use of a degree of intentional force." 481 F. 2d, at 1033. He added that, in determining whether that intentional use of force "crosse[s]" the "constitutional line," a court should look:

> "to such factors as [(1)] the need for the application of force, [(2)] the relationship between the need and the amount of force that was used, [(3)] the extent of in-jury inflicted, and [(4)] whether force was applied in a good faith effort to maintain or restore discipline or maliciously and sadistically for the very purpose of causing harm." *Ibid.*

This statement does not suggest that the fourth factor (malicious and sadistic purpose to cause harm) is a *necessary* condition for liability. To the contrary, the words "such . . . as" make clear that the four factors provide examples of some considerations, among others, that might help show that the use of force was excessive.

Respondents believe these cases nonetheless help them make a broader point—namely, that a subjective standard "protects against a relative flood of claims," many of them perhaps unfounded, brought by pretrial detainees. Brief for Respondents 38. But we note that the Prison Litigation Reform Act of 1995, 42 U. S. C. §1997e, which is designed to deter the filing of frivolous litigation against prison officials, applies to both pretrial detainees and convicted prisoners. Nor is there evidence of a rash of unfounded filings in Circuits that use an objective standard.

We acknowledge that our view that an objective standard is appropriate in the context of excessive force claims brought by pretrial detainees pursuant to the Fourteenth Amendment may raise questions about the use of a subjective standard in the context of excessive force claims brought by convicted prisoners. We are not confronted with such a claim, however, so we need not address that issue today.

III

We now consider the lawfulness of the jury instruction given in this case in light of our adoption of an objective standard for pretrial detainees' excessive force claims. See Part II–A, *supra*. That jury instruction defined "excessive force" as "force applied recklessly that is unreasonable in light of the facts and circumstances of the time." App. 277. It required Kingsley to show that the officers "recklessly disregarded [Kingsley's] safety." *Id.*, at 278. And it suggested that Kingsley must show the defendants "acted with reckless disregard of [Kingsley's] rights," while telling the jury that it could consider several objective factors in making this determination. *Ibid.*

Kingsley argues that the jury instruction is faulty because the word "reckless" suggests a need to prove that respondents acted with a certain subjective state of mind with respect to the excessive or nonexcessive nature of the force used, contrary to what we have just held. Reply Brief 20–22. Respondents argue that irrespective of our holding, any error in the instruction was harmless. Brief for Respondents 57–58. And the Solicitor General suggests that, because the instructions defined "recklessness" with reference to objective factors, those instructions effectively embody our objective standard and did not confuse the jury. Brief for United States as *Amicus Curiae* 28–32.

We agree with Kingsley that the instructions were erroneous. "[R]eckles[s] disregar[d] [of Kingsley's] safety" was listed as an additional requirement, beyond the need to find that "[respondents'] use of force was unreasonable in light of the facts and circumstances at the time." App. 278. See also *ibid.* (Kingsley had to show respondents "used unreasonable force *and* acted with reckless disregard of [Kingsley's] rights" (emphasis added)). And in determining whether respondents "acted with reckless disregard of [Kingsley's] rights," the jury was instructed to "consider . . . [w]hether [respondents] reasonably *believed* there was a threat to the safety of staff or prisoners." *Ibid.* (emphasis added). Together, these features suggested the jury should weigh respondents' subjective reasons for using force and subjective views about the excessiveness of the force. As we have just held, that was error. But because the question whether that error was harmless may depend in part on the detailed specifics of this case, we leave that question for the Court of Appeals to resolve in the first instance.

The decision of the Court of Appeals is vacated, and the case is remanded for proceedings consistent with this opinion.

It is so ordered.

1. In this case, the Supreme Court Justices decided based on using objective versus subjective definitions of "excessive force." What circumstances do you think make use of force subjective and why?

2. One of the precedents cited involves delineating how officers treat those awaiting trial from those who have been convicted. How do you think this might apply as a precedent if a later case comes before the Court involving use of force by officers arresting a suspect?

"*MARYLAND V. KING*: THREE CONCERNS ABOUT POLICING AND GENETIC INFORMATION," BY ELIZABETH E. JOH, FROM *GENOMICS LAW REPORT*, SEPTEMBER 19, 2013

With its decision in *Maryland v. King*, the Supreme Court finally stepped into the debate about the use of DNA databases in the criminal justice system. The United States now has the largest DNA database in the world, with 10.4 million offender profiles and 1.5 million arrestee profiles as of June 2013. In *King*, the Court was called upon to decide whether the Fourth Amendment prohibits the collection of DNA samples from arrestees without a warrant or probable cause, the traditional requirements of searches and seizures.

The majority opinion, written by Justice Kennedy, held that the collection of a DNA sample from an arrestee in these circumstances constituted a reasonable Fourth Amendment search, given the outcome of a balancing of interests between the government and the individual. In a sharply written dissent, Justice Scalia criticized the majority's approval of searches that were conducted specifically for law enforcement purposes yet did not conform to traditional Fourth Amendment requirements.

While *King* affirms that DNA databanking in the criminal justice system is here to stay, the majority opinion, when considered with some of the Court's prior Fourth Amendment decisions, raises at least three potentially troubling concerns about policing and genetic privacy.

First, Justice Kennedy's majority opinion permits the police to use arrests in an instrumental manner to collect DNA samples from those persons whom the police suspect are involved in crimes unrelated to the crime of arrest. Alonzo King himself was arrested for assault, but was later linked to an unsolved rape because of the DNA sample generated from his assault arrest. Maryland police had no idea he was involved in the rape until a match was made in the state DNA database between the crime scene evidence and his sample taken because of his arrest on the unrelated assault. In rejecting King's challenge to his compulsory DNA swab, Justice Kennedy noted that King was not subjected to the whims of police officers motivated by law enforcement interests, because state law required *every* person arrested for a qualifying offense to submit a sample.

While it is true that this aspect of DNA sampling did not permit the police to exercise any discretion, the majority fails to acknowledge an important source of unchecked police decision-making. What if the police have a hunch that a person is involved in crime A, but lack the basis to apply for a warrant to obtain a confirmatory DNA sample? Can they arrest the person for minor crime B for the *purpose* of getting a DNA sample? The answer under the Court's prior decisions here is an unequivocal "yes." In particular, the Court's 1996 decision in *Whren v. United States* makes it clear that so long as the police have probable cause to arrest an individual, their subjective motivations for the arrest cannot be challenged under the Fourth Amendment. Because *King* ignores other possible exercises of police discretion, little protects individuals from being targeted for DNA collection under the guise of an arrest for a minor offense.

This leads to my second concern. A careful reader of *King* might point out that this concern about instrumental policing was already anticipated in the majority opinion. After all, the majority limits its holding to instances when the police arrest an individual for a "serious offense." Justice Scalia's dissent rightly focuses on this limitation. While the state law in question does limit arrestee DNA collection to certain serious crimes, there is little in the majority opinion to prevent legislatures from expanding the pool of eligible arrestees.

The chief culprit here is *King's* balancing test. According to Justice Kennedy, when measured against the "quick and painless" swab of Alonzo King's cheek, the government's "interest in identification" is much weightier. The characterization of the interests here are dubious. King was much more concerned about the information Maryland gleaned from his cheek swab than he was about the brief intrusion into his body. Moreover, if the government's interest in identifying arrestees is critical, why does the gravity of the arrest offense matter?

Legislatures might act upon this desire for more information in two ways. First, they could increase the types of arrestees eligible for compulsory DNA collection to include a larger group of felonies or even minor crimes. (This would follow the pattern of convicted persons, ever-increasing numbers of whom are now required to provide DNA samples.) Second, legislatures might also choose to make more legal violations subject to arrest, rather than only to citation. This would provide the police more opportunities—and thus more discretion—to decide which persons to arrest.

Finally, the *King* decision opens up one possibility that may not be obvious and yet is likely to be an important future issue: *Terry* stops that involve the compulsory collection of DNA. Brief investigative stops and limited searches, sanctioned by the Court in *Terry v. Ohio*, are part of standard police practice. The Supreme Court has made it clear that included within the scope of a legitimate *Terry* stop is an investigation into the suspect's identity. If an investigation into one's identity is an acceptable objective in the *Terry* stop context, the collection of DNA for that purpose would seem to be appropriate even in circumstances short of arrest.

While such "DNA *Terry* stops" are not now a part of routine policing, they may very well be in the near future. The technology for "rapid DNA analysis"—which would provide the police with fully automated DNA analysis outside of a lab—is currently under development. Indeed, the FBI in 2010 established a Rapid DNA Program Office to promote technological standards in the hope of producing a kit that will provide a DNA profile within two hours or less of sample collection.

None of these issues that I have raised here have yet arisen with any urgency. And certainly legislators could act to prevent or restrict some of these scenarios from coming to pass. The truth is, however, that most of the trends suggest the ever greater use of DNA sampling by law enforcement officials: a development that the *King* decision has only made easier.

1. *Maryland v. King* opens a wide door for legal collection of DNA samples from citizens. In addition to the concerns cited above, what other issues do you think may arise from this court decision when it comes to genetic information collected?

2. A related court decision—*Terry v. Ohio*—is cited here. Based on the information given, how do you think Terry stops may play into the issues cited above? Do you think these types of stops should be legal? Why or why not?

CHAPTER 4

WHAT ADVOCACY ORGANIZATIONS SAY

Advocacy organizations are working diligently to investigate any and all matters of alleged police overreach to better understand the current climate in police interactions with the public. In the first selection in this chapter, Damian Ortellado looks into data already being collected by the Centers for Disease Control and Prevention (CDC) to see if there is racial disparity in injury reports resulting from police interactions in an article for the Sunlight Foundation, a nonpartisan organization that advocates for open government.

In the following selection, "When Police Are Part of the Problem of Violence: The Case of Papua New Guinea's Police Force" by Alicia Lynch, the Seeds Theatre Group of Papua New Guinea looks at reported issues with police, showing that these issues are universal, and noting how police forces may have internal issues that impact how they interact with the public.

Finally, Ben Brucato writes for the *American Studies Journal* in "Standing By Police Violence: On the Constitution of the Ideal Citizen as Sousveiller," advocating for greater citizen involvement in recording police interactions with the public acting as "sousveillance," or surveillance from the opposite side.

"EMERGENCY ROOM REPORTS REVEAL RACIAL DISPARITY IN INJURIES CAUSED BY POLICE," BY DAMIAN ORTELLADO, FROM THE SUNLIGHT FOUNDATION, SEPTEMBER 4, 2014

Disturbing video evidence surfaced in July that shows a California Highway Patrol officer aggressively and repeatedly striking the sides of 51-year-old Marlene Pinnock's head. The officer reported that Pinnock, a homeless African American woman who had to be hospitalized after the incident, became "physically combative" after attempting to walk into rush-hour traffic, despite a civil rights lawsuit against the officer that claims otherwise.

While the incident involving Pinnock is alarming, it is not unique. Every year, tens of thousands of people are injured by law enforcement in events that rarely stir the same viral outrage. However, the Centers for Disease Control and Prevention regularly collect data about these incidents, which are classified as nonfatal injuries by law enforcement, from hospital emergency department records.

The data reveal not only a racial disparity in the number of nonfatal injuries caused by law enforcement but also an upward trend in their frequency over the last decade. And in the wake of Michael Brown's killing by a police officer in Ferguson, Mo. last month, a national conversation has begun in force about police brutality disproportionately affecting non-whites throughout the country. These data can contribute directly to that conversation and help people who are seeking solutions to the problem.

Using the available data, a comparison of estimates obtained from the CDC's Web-Based Injury Statistics Query and Reporting System (WISQARS) to national census population counts shows that black people suffered over five times as many nonfatal injuries per capita from law enforcement as white people did cumulatively over the years 2001-2012.

And while the rates of nonfatal injuries to women when compared to men are generally significantly lower, the racial trends hold even within this subset. Using the same injury estimate to population count methodology yields nearly identical comparisons between black women and white women, where black women receive five times the rate of nonfatal injuries caused by law enforcement when compared to white women.

It is important to note that approximately 17 percent of the injury data collected by the CDC has no race or ethnicity assigned to the victims. However, even in the case that all unassigned victims of legal intervention injuries were white, the rate of nonfatal injuries to black people by law enforcement would still be over three times higher than that of white people.

The Police-Public Contact Survey, a population survey released by the Bureau of Justice statistics and conducted in 2008, reveals racial discrepancies in people's experience with law enforcement consistent with CDC data. The survey shows that the percentage of black people who reported experiencing the use or threat of force during their most recent contact with police was nearly three times that of white people.

Even if the assault on Pinnock was an isolated incident, the data point to what could be considered a constant struggle for racial equality in interactions with law enforcement — a struggle that, based on trends, does not appear to be getting any easier for minorities in the last decade. While conclusions drawn from the available information should be scrutinized, access to it may shine light on issues that, without any documentation, would prove difficult to analyze at all.

1. If you were looking at the same data noted in this article, are there any other conclusions you might come to based on the numbers? Explain your reasons.

2. The Sunlight Foundation notes that the number of injuries being reported is on the rise. What reasons do you think might result in that increase and why?

"WHEN POLICE ARE PART OF THE PROBLEM OF VIOLENCE: THE CASE OF PAPUA NEW GUINEA'S POLICE FORCE," BY ALICIA LYNCH, FROM SEEDS THEATRE GROUP, OCTOBER 8, 2014

Poor policing is often cited as one of the main contributing factors in the perpetuation of gender-based violence (GBV) in Papua New Guinea (PNG). In what ways do the police in PNG perpetuate violence against women?

> "Police are under-resourced, under-trained, often corrupt, frequently violent, and largely uninterested in the welfare of women and their rights to justice. Complaints of rape of women by police are commonplace, and they are notoriously rough on their wives. In addition, only 10 per cent of their ranks are female." Source: Article by Jo Chandler of the Lowy Institute

LACK OF COMMITMENT BY POLICE OFFICIALS

The relationship between law enforcement officials and women in Papua New Guinea is fraught with numerous examples of indifferent attitudes and a lack of concern from police for victims of domestic and family violence.

According to a report on Gender and Violence, authored by Chief Inspector Miriam Yawa of the Papua New Guinea Constabulary, female victims of family violence are often discouraged from reporting these incidents and sent away. The excuse given by the police is that it is a family matter to be sorted out by the family. In the cases where the police do intervene, they focus on counselling the parties, only to send them away after.

Findings from research conducted for a report by Child Fund indicates that women interviewed in the Rigo District of the country were overwhelmingly negative about the district police, commenting that they "treat women like criminals", "act like criminals" and "cannot be trusted". The interviewees remarked that police demonstrated a lack of interest in responding to acts of abuse and violence against them and that they were sometimes the very perpetrators of the violence. Going to the police was considered as a last resort, reserved for very serious attacks.

STORIES FROM THE GROUND:

"I heard numerous accounts of police officers ignoring complaints, dismissing women from the police stations, encouraging women to drop charges, not enforcing Interim Protection Orders, or receiving bribes from perpetrators to ignore a case. In some instances, it was the lack of resources, including a vehicle or enough fuel; but more often a lack of commitment that affected police officers ability to investigate cases of violence against women. Even when willing to investigate, the lack of specialization in investigative and forensic skills increases the dependence of police officers on witness testimonies to identify perpetrators and consequently to initiate proceedings, which has its own challenges as there is no victim and witness protection scheme." Source: Special Rapporteur on Violence against women on mission in Papua New Guinea

"It is good to see that men are still in control."
Reaction by a senior police officer to an anti-violence poster that depicted a beaten woman.
Source: Information sheet, Australia's support for Gender Equality in Papua New Guinea

WHEN THE POLICE ARE THE PERPETRATORS: POLICE ABUSE IN PNG

Police abuse of civilian women (and police women) is rampant. There are many documented cases of rape and bribery in exchange for the performance of sexual acts and the commission of violent acts against women, by members of the police force.

In Gender-Based Violence in Papua New Guinea, Trends and Challenges authored by Laura Baines, it seems that many women are fearful of reporting these crimes because they think police may ask them to perform a sexual act. Violence by police officials often takes place at night after their work has ended. Documentation from activities around the Porgera Gold Mine show that the area is a mine bed for this type of activity. Women who are caught trespassing are faced with two decisions: allow the police to take them to the police station or be raped.

STORIES FROM THE GROUND:

"In interviews with Human Rights Watch, girls and women told interviewers about rapes, including pack rape, in police stations, vehicles, barracks, and other locations. In some cases, police carried out rapes in front of witnesses. Witnesses described seeing police rape girls and women vaginally and orally, sometimes using objects such as beer bottles. Girls and women who are street vendors, sex workers, and victims reporting crimes to police, as well as boys and men who engage in homo-sexual conduct, appear to be especially targeted." Source: Making Their Own Rules, Human Rights Watch Report, 2005

LOW POLICE PRESENCE

Low police presence due to a lack of resources is also a major problem in many areas of the country. The Papuan Highlands, an area rife with acts of tribal violence, in which women are disproportionately affected, is one such region. There were virtually no police stationed in this area of the country. According to Child Fund, there are only six village courts to serve 228 villages in the Rigo province. This means that more than half the population lives far distances from the nearest court. To obtain justice they are forced to travel for up to a week and sleep on the roadside.

LEGAL INACTION, INCOMPETENCE AND A LACK OF TRAINING

A police officer interviewed at the Rigo Station for Child Fund, acknowledged that women were afraid and reluc-tant to report incidents to police. Instead, they were more likely to try to resolve the issue through their village mag-istrates, or rely on mediation. Even worse is the fact that many magistrates are not trained in the law. The majority of women cannot afford to pay magistrates and must rely on the police to manage their cases. However, the police often impose fines but do not issue warrants for the arrest of abusers.

Laura Baines also observes that not only do police officials refrain from involving themselves in acts of GBV, but if the matters are investigated, they do not do so adequately and often fail to gather sufficient evidence to convict the accused. Constable Yawa's report on Gender and Violence also echoes similar views. Findings from the report showed a distinct lack of training in the appropriate procedures in taking complaints and in gathering evidence, which could lead to the possibility of proceeding with a prosecution without the presence of the complainant.

A DIRE LACK OF RESOURCES: EMPTY TANKS AND NO TRUCKS

Some police stations are so poorly funded that they are forced to borrow fuel from NGOs in order to pursue criminals. Other stations simply cannot attend to victims due to a lack of vehicles. Radios and computers are luxury items.

In his storybook Crying Meri, Vlad Sokhin reports that in many remote places in the country the police are absent. If a rape or an attack occurs, a woman is required to pay the cost of gasoline for the police to respond and investigate. This cost is often prohibitive and therefore, most rapes and acts of violence go unreported.

One such case occurred in September 2014. A man in the Jiwaka province chopped off his mother-in-law's legs and also maimed another female relative prior to the incident. Police blamed a lack of resources on their inability to pursue the offender. There are many more cases like this one.

STORIES FROM THE GROUND:

"Currently we can't go after the suspect because we have logistical problems. Most of the times we have fuel problems. Sometimes we go around begging people to buy fuel just to attend to their complaints and that has been, that has been really a problem that has been hindering us to carry out our job effectively.

"Violence against women is one of the very big problems we have in this, in Jiwaka. We have more than ten complaints of violence against women a day. As far as our police capacity is concerned we are really unable to really address this problem. I believe my government has been allocating funds for this to support the police but from the ground level from the district level we are not getting that kind of support."

Source: Comments from an Inspector Horum Piamia, PNG Police forced to borrow fuel

WHAT IS THE WAY FORWARD?

EFFECTIVE FUNDING AND PARTNERSHIP

Papua New Guinea's police force is of course, the responsibility of the country's government and also heavily bolstered by funding from multiple external donors. However, police officials at the ground level are floundering without access to basic tools which would enable them to exercise their duties. How are funds allocated?

A special report on police engagement and cooperation attributed much of the responsibility of the paucity of resources to the lack of funding by the PNG Government. Spending on the force has been described as 'stagnant', having failed to keep pace with government spending, which is substantially higher. In addition to this, one of the country's principal donors is the Australian Government, whose support to the force has fluctuated at times over the years.

The commitment of Papua New Guinea's Government in creating a more effective police force is expressed through the 2013 RPNGC Modernisation Programme, a five year programme with a budget of $123 million dollars, designed to rebuild the force and improve service delivery within 40 years. Australia has also reaffirmed its moral and financial commitment to assist the PNG police force and will continue to offer training and technical assistance in the area of institutional and capacity-building. A sound emergency stabilisation plan, along with effective monitoring and allocation of funds and an operative partnership with the Australian Government will need to ensue in order to produce the desired results over time and within the short-term period.

REMOVAL OF IMMUNITY AND THE NEED FOR CLOSE SUPERVISION

Police are also unfortunately protected by immunity, which has had a disastrous impact on their image and reputation and has also contributed to the violation of the rights of many of PNG's citizens. Christof Heyns, UN Special Rapporteur on extrajudicial, summary or arbitrary executions comments that the lack of impunity and an undisciplined police force are major sources of the violence in Papua New Guinea. According to a Human Rights Watch report from 2005, police officials are also largely unsupervised and are not

held accountable for acts of abuse or other criminal activity.
Worse yet, there exists a pervasive culture within the force
which condones and allows this discipline. There are many
instances of officers who become repeat offenders and
commit the same offences for years.

RELEVANT TRAINING AND ACCOUNTABILITY

There are also many recommendations for the provision of
additional training programmes for police personnel. However, notwithstanding the need for continued training in
several key areas which include evidentiary procedures,
investigative methods and ensuring convictions, Papua New
Guinea's police force is reportedly the most highly-trained
force in the Pacific region.

From 2000-2005, AusAid's police project trained about
75% of the force. Since then, funding to the police force
has continued to be provided through the Australian and
New Zealand Governments. Training is clearly not producing
the desired results. Despite widespread exposure to training,
there has been little improvement in the management of acts
of violence against women by police officials and acts of
abuse by officials themselves, continue to persist.

Bruce Grant suggests that the reason for the insig-
nificant effect of training on police behavior is due to
the mismatch of the content of training and education
programmes and the needs of the police force. Programmes
do not adequately address the culture of the police force
nor the very root of the problem – the legitimization of male
violence towards women. Moreover, officers are neither
monitored nor supervised closely to ensure that they
attend training or implement the appropriate techniques
and knowledge in the performance of their duties.

SIGNIFICANT CHALLENGES LIE AHEAD

The challenges faced by the force are not only disciplinary, but are compounded by the lack of a strong institutional framework and a lack of basic resources. The lack of accountability, sanctions and monitoring also remain major hindrances to the adequate functioning of the department. Both the PNG Government as well as other donors must ensure that funds and aid are closely monitored and programmes should be accompanied by sanctions and consequences for officers who do not meet the required standards.

The level of aggression displayed by Papuan civilians is supported and even normalised by the structural and cultural institutions of Papuan society. Unfortunately, the Papuan Constabulary is a microcosm of the wider society and they are not immune to displaying the same kind of irreverence for women and their rights that civilian Papuan men demonstrate. The overarching culture of male dominance, superiority and aggression must be addressed in conjunction with a reformation of the police culture and institutions, if things are to change for the better.

1. This article from Seeds Theatre Group shows that issues with police aren't confined to the United States. What issues do you think Papua New Guinea has in common with the United States? Which issues are different?

2. Cultural values, or mores, are cited here as reasons for problems citizens of Papua New Guinea have with the police. What cultural mores in the United States do you think might contribute to the stories we are hearing now in the news?

"STANDING BY POLICE VIOLENCE: ON THE CONSTITUTION OF THE IDEAL CITIZEN AS SOUSVEILLER," BY BEN BRUCATO, FROM THE *AMERICAN STUDIES JOURNAL*, 2016

[*Editor's Note: Figures are not included with this reprint but can be found with the original article.*]

Individual citizens and social movement organizations document police with video, both serendipitously and deliberately. This documentation is characterized as an intervention, one that not only promises to alter events, but to fulfill civic responsibilities. Simply, video recording police makes one an active citizen, rather than a passive bystander. For instance, at Occupy Wall Street, video recording was a primary and normalized response by pro-testers when police used coercive force against other pro-testers. Their use of video streaming apps to live-broad-cast such events—while chanting "The whole world is watching!"—shows how protesters framed watching as an intercession. The National Police Monitoring and Reporting Project frames citizen documentation of police as a duty, one that produces protective power against police violence. Copwatch "know your rights" training similarly portrays spontaneous filming as an intervention in violent policing. In other cases, however, video documentation is cast as a shame-worthy denial of a citizen's responsibility to intervene to stop the perpetration of violence. In light of its equivocal standing, the treatment of documenting violence as an intervention is in doubt.

This research was supported by the Humanities, Arts, and Social Sciences Fellowship at Rensselaer Polytechnic University and the Center for Humanistic Inquiry at Amherst College. The author thanks Nancy D. Campbell, Martha Umphrey, Kiara M. Vigil, Patricia E. Chu, Matthew Schilleman, and Max Perry Mueller for helpful commentary on earlier drafts; and Andrew Gross for his generous assistance in polishing the manuscript.

THE WHOLE WORLD IS WATCHING

On September 17, 2011, several hundred activists marched to Wall Street in New York City, near the New York Stock Exchange. This group quickly increased in size, including several thousand protestors who took and maintained control of Zuccotti Park. There, campers maintained an ongoing occupation of the park, which served as a microcommunity and home to dozens of permanent campers, and hundreds who stayed for varying lengths of time (Brucato, 2012). This space became known as Occupy Wall Street and inspired a global Occupy movement. One of the Occupy Wall Street protesters, Felix Rivera-Pitre, is HIV+ and was living on a $300 per month income at the YMCA in Jamaica Queens during the occupation. At a march through the streets of Manhattan on October 14, 2011, New York Police Department (NYPD) Officer Johnny Cardona ordered Rivera-Pitre to move from the street to the sidewalk. Seconds later, Cardona punched Rivera-Pitre, knocking him to the ground. Rivera-Pitre explains, "The cop just lunged at me full throttle and hit me on the left side of my face" (Robbins). Several videos posted on YouTube documented the assault and show Cardona and Rivera-Pitre surrounded by dozens of people, most all of them holding video cameras or cellphones (see e.g., "NYPD White Shirt").

A blogger for *San Francisco Chronicle*'s website reported on the incident, remarking, "Cell phones and social media are the great equalizers in keeping law enforcement accountable…With everyone in the vicinity carrying cell phones, hundreds of cameras were pulled out during the chaos and the streets were filled with chants of: 'THE WHOLE WORLD IS WATCHING!'" (Leon).

There is nothing exceptional about this incident. In the first month of Occupy Wall Street, hundreds of occupiers and marchers were arrested, and perhaps as many or more were assaulted by police without being arrested. In most instances, protesters with cameras surrounded the police chanting, "The whole world is watching! The whole world is watching!" This became so routine such that each new instance was a rehearsal for the next. The media produced in these moments communicate a message about normalized responses to the presence of police violence. Bystanders fulfill the function of documenting the perpetration of violence and circulating their media to exhibit evidence of wrongdoing. Because these incidents were so common, and because they were documented by dozens—sometimes hundreds—of cameras, many thousands of images circulated these spectacles. Though news crews were often present at Occupy events, news producers were keen to televise amateur video content. The amateur images conveyed a sense of authenticity, and offered an almost limitless access to any time or vantage point—all at no cost to the station, with no licensing granted by the producers of the images or releases signed by the subjects. Because Occupy had become a media event, networks provided expanded access to activists and police to be exhibited through traditional channels.

In the image of Occupy Wall Street below (Figure 1), it appears that there are more people with cameras than without. In the video from which I selected this still, the crowd is heard chanting and shaming the officers after they tackled the bearded man in the black hat and blue mask, near the center of the frame.

The chant rang out: "The whole world is watching! The whole world is watching!"—referencing the antici-pated immediacy of documentary video and photography reaching a worldwide audience. It was not that the whole world will see, but that the world is watching. Though few public spectacles automatically become immediate internet spectacles, Occupy Wall Street quickly garnered such status and maintained it for many months. Users posted and shared documents on websites like YouTube, Flickr, Facebook, Twitter and other social media applica-tions, and the hashtag #OWS all but assured rapid recir-culation. Armed with knowledge of quasi-immediate social sharing, the crowd imagined a world of viewers who became telepresent. This telepresence suggests that at the moment of the application of force against protesters by police, the events had gone live to a global audience that was poised to watch. Furthermore, Occupy Wall Street popularized video streaming applications for smart phones, like LiveStream and Ustream. Using these apps, amateur journalists and activists armed with nothing but a cellphone could provide live video, televised over the internet. Links to these video streams were Tweeted with the #OWS hashtag so remote viewers could locate them and tune in.

STANDING BY POLICE VIOLENCE IN A SURVEILLANCE SOCIETY

By November 2011, many thousands of protesters and occupiers were arrested at Occupy events around the country (Brucato, 2012). Countless arrests were documented by professional and amateur journalists, but also by independent activists, media activist collectives, and cop watch groups—often simultaneously. Fernandez explains that emerging legal, physical, and psychological processes used by the state—especially since September 11, 2001, and in the United States—have intensified the governmental monitoring and suppression of dissent. Crucial to these developments has been the use of repression by police against protesters. Not only have the cameras of professional journalists documented police crowd control tactics and efforts to physically control space; so too have the amateur journalists, independent activists and organized cop watch groups monitoring the protests. Consequently, documentations have been created and disseminated without the editorial filters employed by corporate news agencies. Before the Occupy movement, protest policing was once only visible during rare though momentous anti-globalization protests, seldom lasting more than a day or two. Though Occupy Wall Street initially received little national media attention by mainstream news outlets, amateur journalists and media activists circulated visual documentation on social media sites. A media team formed by the protesters at Zuccotti Park edited and uploaded footage, and video streaming apps achieved new visibility and use as protesters broadcast Occupy events over mobile broadband signals to live audiences. Especially at Occupy Wall Street, and particularly after the mainstream media began covering the occupations, the Occupy movement provided new visibility of protest policing. For the first time in decades, large scale policing tactics became apparent in daily news coverage that lasted for months.

Around the same time as Occupy Wall Street, videos documenting everyday police violence began to proliferate. On January 1, 2009, dozens of witnesses watched BART (Bay Area Rapid Transit) Police Officer Johannes Mehserle shoot Oscar Grant in the back, killing him while another officer restrained him, prone on a train platform in Oakland, California. The incident was video recorded by several of these witnesses. In Manteca, California, on June 8, 2011, Officer John Moody's dashboard mounted camera recorded him shooting to death Ernesto Duenez, Jr. On July 5, 2011, municipal CCTV (closed-circuit television) cameras recorded Fullerton Police Department Officers Manuel Ramos and Jay Cicinelli beating Kelly Thomas into a coma. Thomas died five days later.

On August 9, 2014, in Ferguson, Missouri, an on-duty white police officer, Darren Wilson, shot and killed an unarmed 18-year-old Black man, Michael Brown.

This incident captured the attention and inspired the mobilization of existing activists and organizations across the country under the #BlackLivesMatter banner. While Brown's killing was not captured on video, around this time several others were, adding fuel to a surging movement. On July 17, 2014, Eric Garner was recorded on a cellphone video by a civilian as he was choked and suffocated by New York Police Department Officer Daniel Pantaleo. Likewise, a civilian recorded Charly "Africa" Leundeu Keunang as he was shot and killed by a LAPD Sgt. Chand Syed and Officers Francisco Martinez and Daniel Torres in February 2015. Another cellphone video showed Walter Scott being shot and killed by North Charleston Police Officer Michael T. Slager in April 2015. These examples are among dozens of videos documenting police killings and easily found on YouTube and other websites like LiveLeak that host user-supplied video content.

Modern police power has always been articulated through managing its own visibility while making those selected for police scrutiny available to surveillance. Brighenti explains this command over visibility is an exemplary type of surveillance, where police rely on a metaphoric "unseen seeing eye" (154). Surveillance etymologically—'sur–' meaning 'over' and 'veillance,' 'watching'—suggests a comparatively powerful entity watching over the actions of subordinated persons (Mann, Nolan, and Wellman).

This watching can be understood as a response to the possibilities of concealment offered by modern cities. David Lyon (2001) explains that the disappearance of individual bodies has been a basic problem of modernity, a consequence of increasingly complex social organization and populations increasing in size and density. This sense of being lost in the metropolis was a dominant theme in the modern era, and was addressed by authors like Edgar Allen Poe in the mid-nineteenth century, by sociologists like Georg Simmel at the turn of the twentieth century, and by philosophers like Walter Benjamin two decades later.

Powerful institutions and the privileged actors therein—like police agencies and their officers—have access to technologies, techniques, and institutions that make bodies reappear, and in doing so enable control over these bodies for the purposes of direction, protection, and administration (Lyon, 2001). The methods of making bodies visible are various, but the effect of such surveillance is to render the body as an object of classification and record (Bruno; Crary; Sekula). The broadly shared experience of being watched has been normalized, such that publics have internalized the surveillant gaze of the state (Marx; Foucault). Complying with laws and social norms is partly a result of feeling one is being watched even if the watchers are not apparent. This is the most fundamental aspect of the panopticon metaphor: that publics subconsciously recognize the possibility of being watched at any moment and so feel compelled to comply at all times (Lyon, 2006). Panoptic surveillance is an attempt at an efficient solution when total transparency is infeasible, a solution intended to manufacture voluntary submission to regulation. Nonetheless, in a surveillance society, "it is increasingly difficult for individuals to maintain their anonymity, or to escape the monitoring of social institutions," leading to what Haggerty and Ericson call "the disappearance of disappearances" (619).

Mathiesen's concept of the synopticon explains the inversion of the literal meaning of surveillance, where instead the many watch the few. Goldsmith finds that Mathiesen's "viewer society" underscores the incidental and unintentional aspects of participation in watching. Kearon explains that from the late 1980s onward is "a period in which the traditional state monopoly of access to surveillance technologies has been eroded, with a growing range of widely accessible technologies that can be utilized by the public to carry out informal surveillance" (413). Policing's new visibility is especially a result of "the capacity of these technologies in the hands of ordinary citizens and residents to alter the public visibility of policing and thereby to impact upon public perceptions of policing and challenge existing mechanisms for police accountability" (Goldsmith 916).

Sousveillance is a term used by surveillance scholars to call attention to this informal surveillance as historically and analytically unique. The term is an etymological antonym for surveillance, where 'sous-,' or 'under,' 'inverts' the perspective from which watching takes place (Yesil). Mann and colleagues define sousveillance very specifically as "the recording of an activity by a participant in the activity," one that "decentralizes observation to produce transparency in all directions," but is nonetheless serendipitous in quality (177).

In American cities, segregation has been a constant, and those neighborhoods with few white citizens are most intensively policed and surveilled (Brucato, 2014). Residents in these communities are used to seeing police violence, while those outside these communities are newly exposed as a consequence of proliferating cameras, whether mounted in police vehicles or carried in the pockets of civilians. Police once had both legal authority and technical ability to autonomously modulate its visibility, but in describing what he calls "policing's new visibility," Goldsmith explains "the conditions of choice open to police organizations and personnel in this regard have been eroded dramatically in recent years as a consequence of new communicative technologies and their social use" (915).

This means, among other things, that disguising or hiding unflattering, illegal or other behavior contrary to community norms is not as fully within the command of officers and agencies. Police have always had to manage a precarious relationship with various publics, but "impression management is less within the control of the police or indeed government authorities than before" (Goldsmith 917). According to Goldsmith, public contro-versies following use-of-force incidents may undermine police-civilian relations, which can in turn interfere with voluntary submission to criminal laws or compliance with investigations. Additionally, the visibility of "less flattering or illegal practices" exposes officers and agencies to disciplinary and legal liability (Goldsmith 915).

Some predict that legal and other accountability processes for police misconduct may become superfluous as police visibility to cameras reaches ubiquity. Recent studies of police visibility suggest a reversal of the panop-ticon, where police officers will internalize the expectation of being under constant scrutiny by civilians, and so will self-regulate (Ariel, Farrar, and Sutherland; Newell). Such a view treats the power of cameras as transferable, emerging from visibility itself. However, it might make more sense to see them as tools used to concentrate, amplify, or organize authority that pre-exists their deployment. The panopticon model functions because the self-regulating persons are inside prison cells, monitored by guards armed with truncheons and the authority to legitimately use violence to control the prison population.

While researchers equivocate as to whether cameras have produced a "civilizing effect" in police behavior toward civilians (White), we do know that police engage in "counter-sousveillance" measures in order "to deter persons from filming [police] and, if unsuccessful, even to seize cameras and recorders believed to contain unflattering images of police activities" (Goldsmith 929). Though such efforts are common, the U.S. Department of Justice has clarified that video recording police is protected by the First Amendment (Borja). Furthermore, most seizures of civilian cameras constitute a Fourth Amendment violation. Using some contents on cellphones to incriminate their owners could also constitute a Fifth Amendment violation. A more technical and sophisticated counter-sousveillance strategy is evinced in the development, marketing, and rapid adoption of officer-worn cameras by police agencies. These cameras are intended to take advantage of the legally and culturally privileged perspective of officers, particularly when they use violent force (Brucato, 2015). Essentially, these cameras produce surveillance footage intended to nullify sousveillance footage.

Despite new efforts by police to manage and control their visibility in an era of ubiquitous surveillance, civilians are increasingly inclined to create and share videos documenting their on-the-job behaviors. The proliferating amateur video archive is evidence of a normalizing activity, showing that recording police is becoming institutionalized, a set of self-activating sequential technical and social actions that bystanders perform, deliberately or otherwise.

"WE ARE ALL BYSTANDERS NOW"

Mann and colleagues' definition of sousveillance points to the significance of the bystander recording an event with a smartphone. As a consequence of proliferating sousveillance and the broad diffusion and use of such mobile information and communication technologies, Bauman contends that it is increasingly difficult for one to legitimately claim ignorance of suffering, no matter how near or far the sufferer is, and so "we are all bystanders now." This now pervasive problem was impetus for Bauman to revisit the taken-for-granted causal relationship between bystander non-intervention and the perpetuation of suffering. Traditionally, perpetrators are identified by their "doing evil," whether in violation of law or community norms. According to Bauman, bystanders are identified by offering "non-resistance to evil." Bystanders know that something needs to be done, but they also know that other bystanders have done less than has been needed. This rationalization has the effect of absolving the bystander of any definite responsibility to act.

The problem of the bystander highlights a conflict between the humanitarian responsibility to prevent suffering on the one hand, and the rational and irrational fears about the consequences of intervention on the other (Milgram & Hollander). Even when bystander apathy presents no grounds for legal action or social stigma, it is nonetheless causally linked to past and ongoing victimization. As Bauman argues, "refraining from action carries a causal load not much lighter than acting, while the certainty (or high probability) of general non-resistance by the non-lookers may carry a heavier responsibility for the ill actions and their effects than the mere presence of a number of ill-intentioned villains" (Bauman 140–41). Because of the global expansion of information and communication technologies, distance is no longer an excuse for lack of knowledge about victimization and suffering, and, according to Bauman, offers no reliable rationale for inaction. Further, global trends in ethics show an expansion of moral concern for all of humanity—and increasingly beyond, i.e., to non-human animals. These coinciding changes mean that "the gap between things *done* and things *to be done* seems to be swelling instead of shrinking" (Bauman 143, italics in original).

The bystander effect refers to a theory—with some empirical support—about the apathy of non-involved parties. Most crucially, the theory suggests the diffusion of responsibility, specifically an inverse relationship between the likelihood of a non-involved person intervening to stop the victimization of another person and the number of other witnesses. A famous study by Latané and Darley identifies the "bystander syndrome" as a situation in which onlookers lack the will to act but are nonetheless compelled to keep watching. While their research is flawed due to factual errors and weak empirical support for its general applicability (Gallo), this framing of watching and (not) acting is useful for the present inquiry. Bauman in particular has critically mobilized this analytical frame in the context globalization and informatization: now that responsibility is as diffuse as ever, both the capacity and the impulse to act seem as minimal as ever. The Occupy Wall Street protesters who recorded and chanted at police demonstrate that in this context, one's responsibility to act is provided with a particularly ironic option to watch. Acting, in other words, becomes a way of diffusing responsibility with the expectation of amplifying the power of intervention. The protesters are not alone in this expectation, as it guides a wide range of arguments about ideal responses for witnesses to police violence.

TELEPHONE OPERATORS ARE STANDING BY

The Cato Institute's National Police Misconduct Reporting Project (NPMRP) describes itself as "a non-governmental, non-partisan independent project that will attempt to determine the extent of police misconduct in the United States, identify trends affecting police misconduct, and report on issues about police misconduct in order to enhance public awareness on issues regarding police misconduct in the U.S" (National Police Misconduct Reporting Project). In addition to these activities, they publish lectures and written "know your rights" materials. Through their "If You See Something, Film Something" ad campaign, the NPMRP communicates the imperative for civilians to document police.

In one image used in the campaign—and sold as bumper stickers on the NPMRP website—the main text reads, "If you see something, film something!" and below it, "The power to fight police abuse is in your hands." To the right of this text is a drawing of a hand holding a cellphone. The NPMRP uses the imperative mood to command an activity of the viewer: if people see "police abuse," then they should record it with their cellphone cameras. This conveys a responsibility, suggesting that video recording police is an appropriate and necessary response.

This seemingly simple ad consolidates a host of discourses from the contemporary context. First, the campaign uses language and design elements from the U.S. Department of Homeland Security's (DHS) "If You See Something, Say Something" ad campaign. The DHS commands citizens to "say something," compelling them to act as the eyes and ears of the state, reporting back relevant information to aid in securitization. As such, the image directly signals its context in a surveillance society. Second, the message functions in a political world in which spectacle and visuality are central. As Green asserts, whereas classic democracies relied upon the voice of the people, contemporary democracy relies on their eyes. The switch from "say something" to "film something" signifies this shift from speech to vision. Political contentions are frequently situated around images, and today struggles for visibility are fundamental to the assertion of power (Thompson). Third, this discourse functions through the affordances of technologies that have become central to everyday life. Cellphones with cameras, internet connectivity, and social media apps produce communicative capacities and provide the mediums through which contemporary U.S. civilians imagine they can have access to and communicate within civic spaces. The drawing of the camera calls on its symbol as a generator of images with special personal, social, and political salience. The sense that producing and sharing video grants special significance to an event—and one's presence within it and experience of it—is exemplified in the reference to "power" in the secondary message: the cell phone grants power to the person holding it. That power can "fight police abuse."

Another ad in the same campaign reaffirms this message. The main text in this image is identical to the first, but the secondary text reads, "Help prevent police misconduct before you become a victim—It's not just your right, it's your duty." In this more complex message, the NPMSR claims citizens are required to record the police. A threat is suggested in this second image: it is inevitable that the viewer will eventually fall victim to police violence—unless she stops it first. Importantly here, filming the police is not just a fight against police misconduct. It is supposed to prevent present police violence and a future assault that would have otherwise been inflicted on the viewer of the graphic.

By seemingly addressing a universal audience, the ad minimizes the racialized quality of police violence in the United States. Further, it obscures the fact that filming does not directly prevent but at most helps to prevent police misconduct. The means by which to perform this preventive aid is absent in the message, suggesting that video recording alone initiates a self-activating process of prevention.

Above the text in this second ad are 23 still images, mostly derived from cellphone videos shot by civilians. The largest still, featured prominently in the center, comes from a video shot on January 1, 2009, in Oakland, California. In this scene, at least two officers are restraining an unarmed Black man, Oscar Grant, prostrate on a Bay Area Rapid Transit (BART) train platform. I have described the shooting of the restrained man above. The number of images on this graphic amplifies the impor-tance of filming, but it also undercuts the preventative message. If filming police violence prevents the present and future occurrence of police brutality and killings, then how is it that so many of these images could have been created for inclusion in the ad?

The pro-sousveillance message suggests a self-activating accountability process that implicitly relies on more factors than the presence of video (Goldsmith; Brucato, 2015). Also, the priority for producing quality footage requires that bystanders be physically passive, perhaps even silent. Nevertheless, through invoking civic responsibility—"It's not just your right, it's your duty"—the ideal citizen is presented as a sousveiller. The production of mediated visibility is presented as wholly positive and the fulfillment of a public duty. In the next section on best sousveillance practices, I will show how similar messages are communicated by video activists.

HOW TO STAND BY

Carlos Miller founded in 2007 and runs the organization Photography Is Not A Crime! (PINAC). Chiefly, the organization functions as a blog at photographyisnotacrime.com, and it promotes the rights of photographers and videographers to record in public space, especially when documenting public officials. Two key component of PINAC's advocacy are promoting professional models for amateur journalism and providing publicity for journalists—among whom PINAC includes cop watchers—arrested in the course of their work. Together, PINAC's work promotes copwatching but also narrows its strategies in important ways. In Miller's "Ten Rules for Recording Cops," he advises acting as a documenter of events: "you need to think of yourself as a journalist, not an activist" (Miller). To provide the best documentations, Miller suggests obtaining a quality video camera. Beyond its ability to produce better quality video than a cellphone, a dedicated video camera provides the practical benefit of leaving the user with a phone in the event the camera is confiscated by police—legally or otherwise. An advantage smart phones have over dedicated cameras is the ability to use live stream-ing apps (e.g. Bambuser, Qik, and Ustream) to automatically protect footage on cloud storage.

Miller's first rule is "learn to hold the camera." Proper handling includes standing still to minimize obstructions and camera movement, and using both hands to reduce camera shake. In order to ensure the best quality video, one must forego other actions. This precludes interven-tion, essentially turning oneself into a bystander. It further demonstrates an affiliation with the audience rather than with the person being victimized. While that audience might be leveraged, *post facto*, to support the needs of a victim, this signifies, at most, a deferral of intervention. This affiliation is reasserted in the second rule, "keep your mouth shut […] it's more important to capture what is taking place so make that your priority" (Miller). The anonymous audience benefits from the videographer's presence by being able to "form their own opinion." Another rule claims a sousveiller's goal ought to be "transparency." Transparency, here, is modeled on "the fundamental ethics of journalism," "presenting the facts and allowing our followers to form their own opinions" (Miller). The quality of documentation in this journalistic model is one that strives toward accuracy, replicating for the viewer the visible experience of an event.

Most of Miller's other rules pertain to requirements to learn various laws and regulations in order to assert one's right to film under various conditions. This aspect of the guidelines replicates the "know your rights" training events popularized by Copwatch organizations since the 1990s. These organizations are principally identified by coordinating and conducting "patrols" to document traffic and other police stops. They often select for their patrols neighborhoods that are treated by police as "high crime" zones. Because of this, patrols have been most visible and active in neighborhoods populated primarily by people of color.

David Whitt lives in the housing projects in Ferguson, Missouri, where Michael Brown was killed by Officer Darren Wilson on August 9, 2014. Despite not having an activist history, after the killing he began political organizing (D. Whitt, personal communication, October 14, 2014). Whitt was protesting the killing but also engaging in efforts to respond constructively to what he saw as a pattern of excessive force, particularly against people of color. He founded the Canfield Watchmen, who with the support of a crowd-funded campaign by We Copwatch, distributed over one hundred wearable video cameras to Ferguson residents. In distributing these cameras, the Watchmen conduct training events to promote the serendipitous and planned documentation of police by individuals in their community. The group also engages in copwatch patrols, where members seek out and document police stops and arrests.

Kristian Williams asserts that "a broadly based, if informal, practice of copwatching demonstrates public suspicion of the police, normalizes the community's right to observe the police [...]" (Williams). Before disbanding, Rose City Copwatch, founded by Williams, conducted regular training events for residents of Portland, Oregon, in which activists would "run through a bunch of role plays, presenting the participants with real-world scenarios, including facing hostile cops, over-friendly cops, and arrestees who are confused about what the Copwatchers are doing." The Canfield Watchmen and Rose City Copwatch are activist responses to police violence that privilege documentation. Though they suggest that using video to record police is effective response in its own right, this activist model is thoroughly bound up with political organizing and agitation on behalf of those victimized by police. This is further demonstrated in some Copwatch organizations' training to strategically deescalate police violence.

The affiliation of the videographer is less overtly partisan in the journalistic model, which differs from the activist orientation advanced by the Canfield Watchmen and Copwatch groups. The journalistic approach encourages an affiliation with an undifferentiated audience, and so the imperative is to produce the most accurate documentation possible. As such, this model constitutes the ideal sousveiller as passive. Miller, of PINAC, privileges the public's presumed right to know and advocates releasing footage to the public. In doing so, he subordinates concerns about the consent of those victimized by police or about whether the evidence would be criminally or otherwise damaging to them—a matter of paramount concern for most Copwatch groups. For Miller, videographers are left to determine for themselves whether to share footage to police, but are instructed to archive the footage and to "post online anything you have shared with them [police] in order to remain transparent" (Miller). Most Copwatch

groups refuse to aid police in an investigation unless legally
compelled. Nonetheless, what both models share is a belief
that sousveillance constitutes an ideal response for those
in the presence of police violence.

THE SHAME OF THE BYSTANDER

Latané and Darley's research on bystanders in the 1970s
responded to a popular obsession with the case of
Kitty Genovese. On March 13, 1964, Genovese was stalked,
assaulted, and eventually killed by a stranger while she
screamed for help to dozens of bystanders who watched,
mostly from the windows of their apartments in Queens,
New York. In the popular—though disputed—telling of
the story, none of the bystanders phoned police or physically intervened, though a few shouted to the perpetrator
to stop (Manning, Levine, and Collins; Gallo). For decades,
the story has been used as an example in psychology
texts to evaluate and explain the causes of bystander
non-intervention. The story also functions as a parable,
told to shame bystanders for apathy and to thus encourage intervention.

Like the bystanders of the Genovese incident, in
1991, Roger Holliday watched the beating of Rodney King
by Los Angeles Police Department (LAPD) officers from
his apartment. In this incident, Holliday covertly recorded
a video that Mann and colleagues refer to as "probably
the best-known recent example of sousveillance" (Mann,
Nolan, and Wellman 333). Yesil explains the lasting significance of the Rodney King video, writing it "has served
as one of the first and most widely-viewed examples of
the power of mobile recorded image. The message of

the Rodney King tape was that no person, institution or organization was immune from being monitored" (280). The tape's power, she argues, was a function of its wide dissemination, which generated unprecedented public awareness about police violence.

On July 17, 2014, without any prior expectation of documenting police activity, Ramsey Orta recorded New York Police Department officers with his cellphone just as they began killing Eric Garner in Staten Island. On a similarly serendipitous occasion, Feidin Santana made a video of Michael Slager, an on-duty police officer in North Charleston, South Carolina, shooting Walter Scott in the back. Both men have been broadly described as heroes. For instance, Jonathan Capehart of *The Washington Post* wrote:

> Heroes of conscience are rare. Those everyday people who, despite considerable risk to personal safety or their livelihood or both, put themselves in harm's way to expose a larger truth. Feidin Santana is one of them. And it was an honor this morning to shake his hand and call him a hero. (Capehart)

The risk videographers encountered is certainly not disputed. Orta was arrested shortly after recording the killing of Eric Garner. While he was jailed, he reported death threats from guards and engaged in a hunger strike out of fear that his meals would be poisoned. He has since been arrested on two other occasions, which Orta and family members describe as retaliation by police for publicizing the killing of Garner and the ensuing controversy.

The bystanders who watched Genovese's death were widely criticized for their passivity. The men who recorded Garner's and Scott's deaths have been praised for their heroic activity. Their actions did not prevent the violence, but it did bring shame upon the perpetrators. Chanting "The Whole World Is Watching" was likewise expected to function a shaming technique. The witnesses to police violence at Occupy Wall Street anticipated the judgment of the watching world—and that its shame would not turn toward them as it did to Genovese's bystanders. The power of this watching public to shame and thus hold police accountable was presumed to not only provide the possibility of intervention but to be an intervention itself: in recognizing the power of viewers and of viewing, officers were expected to alter their behavior. The crowd used the chant as a means to demand the officers stop what protesters saw as an abuse of authority, a violation of rights, and an infliction of unnecessary suffering. The chant called upon anonymous viewers as a source of the legitimacy for their demand to the police. If the moral fortitude and sheer numbers of the people in the crowd was not enough to convince the officers to cease their assaults, then surely an entire world looking scornfully on their behavior was to be sufficient.

The broadcast images were expected to provide direct access in a much more literal way. Jane Feuer's concept of "liveness" refers to "the ideology of the live, the immediate, the direct, the spontaneous, the real" (14). This concept refers not only to the sense that live broadcast television fosters the "equation of 'the live' and 'the real'" (14), but to the way all television begins to seem "live" and "real" as a result. Streaming video bypasses the filtering of editorial staffs and other corporate controls of mass media, further exaggerating the "live" quality of the televisual. The presumably objective amateur digital image carries a testimonial realism, in part bolstered by its indexical relationship to an event.

Indeed, I would argue that these "live" and indexical qualities are imagined to transform the having-been-there to a being-here. Video streaming contributes to the impression of a colocation of the viewer and the event. Through its testimonial realism, the recorded, archived event lives in the image and can testify for the videographer as a witness. It also testifies to the presence of a crowd of viewer-witnesses. The camera-enabled cell phone and its data connection seems to provide both transparency and telepresence. These qualities are essential for populating the watching world with viewers who cannot help but follow Susan Sontag's command not to turn away from victims of violence.

Through the repetition of such scenes, laden as they are with the chants of crowds shaming officers, these performances take on the form of moral guidance: this is what bystanders ought to do. However, the documentation of perpetration does not seem to *categorically* pass muster as an acceptable intervention. In September 2013, SEPTA (Southeastern Pennsylvania Transportation Authority) Police Officer Samuel Washington was knocked to the ground and struck by Ernest Hays as seven bystanders watched (Cushing). SEPTA Police Chief Thomas Nestel said he was "horrified" and "frightened for my cops" because he could not count on civilians to come to the aid of police officers in distress. One person used her phone to make a video of the assault. Rather than call the documenter a hero, Chief Nestel said, "My immediate thought was 'Shame on you. Why don't you use that phone to call 911?" (Lanier).

On October 20, 2012, Elisa Lopez fell asleep on a New York subway train and woke up to a stranger, Carlos Chuva, groping her (Farberov). Lopez punched the assailant in defense and fled the train (Filipovic). "I stood there for a minute, like, 'What just happened?'" Lopez says. "I see some guy staring at me and the doors closed and the train left. I started crying, because I realized no one helped when this guy did something to me" (Filopovic). Days later, her coworkers saw a video of Lopez's assault on the pornography section of a file-sharing site (Oliver). Lopez was unaware the incident was recorded. Soon, the video appeared on television news. In her discussion of the video, Oliver wrote, "Rather than help her, some bystander took a video and posted it online." Though the video eventually aided in the arrest of Chuva, this after-the-fact response is treated as something other than help. Indeed, Lopez felt more traumatized by the circulation of the video than the assault. News commentators relayed Lopez's sense that the documenter was shame-worthy for failing to provide needed aid. The man who recorded the incident, Jasheem Smiley, posted a video on his YouTube channel defending his actions, claiming there were ten other witnesses who did nothing, that he verbally attempted to wake Lopez, and that he did not physically intervene for fear for his own safety (Farberov).

Beyond feeling abandoned to her own fate by the bystanders, Lopez was also traumatized by the video because it was used by viewers as a source of entertainment. A particular mode of spectatorship, the pornographic gaze, is uniquely conceptualized by Oliver through her reading of Patricia Williams. This voyeurism is grounded in valuing the seen only on the basis of the pleasure the object of vision can provide for the viewer. The pornographic seer is a partisan for his own interests, and particularly his titillation. He disregards the exploitation of those he watches, but, most importantly for Oliver, "the voyeur is not concerned with the effect of his watching on his object" (157).

Those who promote videography as a form of activism argue that watching can have a positive effect. Sedgwick admits that this is sometimes the case, but she also provides a note of caution:

> Some exposés, some demystifications, some bearings of witness do have great effectual force (though often of an unanticipated kind). Many that are just as true and convincing have none at all, however; and as long as that is so, we must admit that the efficacy and directionality of such acts reside somewhere else than in their relation to knowledge per se. (141)

To consider documentation and exhibition as an intervention, as an action that moves a person beyond the position of being a passive (or titillated) spectator, one must demonstrate "effectual force." Are the advocates of sousveillance correct in arguing that videography can provide an effective intervention in a situation of violence?

IGNORANCE, IMPOTENCE, INTERVENTION

As Bauman argues, globalization has destabilized moral frameworks and taken the force out of moral judgments. There are thus a number of strategies that "can easily accommodate all the variety of most commonly used arguments" used to assign blame to bystanders (139). He explains that what Cohen calls "denial" is effective on two levels: the level of ignorance and the level of impotence.

Denial first resorts to a lack of knowledge about wrong-doing: I did not know. The advocates for sousveillance presume that an increase in visibility of wrong-doing, provided by video, has a positive value because it works against ignorance. It is widely recognized—whether in contemporary media studies or among modal consumers of media—that images are not guarantees of physical truth or signifiers with stable meaning (Mitchell). Nevertheless, those who recommend documenting police violence presume this guarantee and stability. The idea that "seeing is believing" seems increasingly wedded to the belief that "sunlight is the best disinfectant." The expectations for publicity of official wrong-doing has increasingly encouraged popular participation in the production of transparency (Brucato, 2015b). This practical participation is clearly aimed at taking away denial as an avenue of retreat—even as it transforms watching into an active rather than a passive activity.

As we saw above, live broadcasted and raw, unedited video is intended to combat ignorance. This tactic is troubled by the fact that the world that watches is not a singular audience. Despite widely held expectations and hopes that media will create or has already fostered a "global village," heterogeneous audiences and the plural objects of their vision are differentiated by their symbolic repertoires. Citing Kapuscinski, Bauman explains "the absorption of *images* may thwart rather than prompt and facilitate the assimilation of *knowledge*. It may also bar the *understanding* of what has been noted and retained, let alone penetrate its causes" (144, italics in original). The prevailing hope for overcoming these facts reinforces what Cheliotis refers to as "narcissistic sensibilities and practices, either by presuming that the included already possess a kind-heartedness in wait only for specific directions, or by framing 'others' as human only insofar as their stories reflect our own emotional world" (172). Here we see a connection across "a truly abysmal gap" between knowing and acting (Bauman 145). Bauman explains that if this "argument from ignorance" fails to be credible—which it is increasingly more likely to do in an era of information exuberance—an "argument from impotence comes to the rescue" (139). This is Cohen's "second-tier" of denial. This argument relies on a rational-choice logic, in which would-be-interveners explain their passivity on the grounds that action would have been ineffectual anyway.

Let us return to the opening example from October 14, 2011, in which Occupy Wall Street protester, Felix Rivera-Pitre, was punched repeatedly by NYPD Officer Johnny Cardona. Dozens of cameras—held by people chanting, "The whole world is watching! The whole world is watching!"—encircled the assault. This group of monitors was joined by two other contingents. The first was comprised by other NYPD officers who attempted to arrest Rivera-Pitre. In the second were bystanders who acted differently from the documenters. Rivera-Pitre describes the scene, saying "The cops were pulling me by my feet and the crowd was pulling me by my hands, and I was suspended in the air" (Robbins). Though he was beaten by those in this first group, the second successfully "de-arrested" Rivera-Pitre, as he escaped into the crowd with their help.

As Goldsmith explains, for police "video is the new reality," and yet it appears little has changed about police violence. Images of police assaulting Occupy Wall Street protesters proliferated. The repetition of these spectacles serves as evidence of the failure of the expectations that these images are, themselves, interventions. Not only did the officers in the documented situations continue to abuse while and after being chanted at by protesters—and, presumably, the watching world—but the spectacle was also repeated thousands of times at Occupy events in the United States. Similarly, in 1992, few would have expected the police institution to recover from the regular repetition of a Rodney King event. Yet today, not a month goes by without a new video circulating that depicts an unarmed Black man beaten or killed by police.

Bauman points out that the technologies that promise a "global village" do not necessarily transcend existing social and spatial divisions. Integral to media is the temporal and spatial separation between those represented and their audiences, and this gap practically disallows intervention. In its colloquial sense, intervention signifies an action to prevent or alter an event, to cause a delay, or physically obstruct something or someone. Etymologically, intervene means to come between. Intervention is identical with interference, meddling, and interruption. Documenting Rivera-Pitre's beating while chanting in anticipation of the shame that viewers would express at the sights they were broadcasting, photographers and videographers claimed to be intervening. However, their spectatorship relegated Rivera-Pitre to be among the past victims of police violence and repression. Though they surrounded him, their action was a non-action, and so their presence was a non-presence. Just like their audiences, they were separated from the event by screens. While documentation may have aided subsequent complaints or legal action, to refer to a promise for a future alteration is to desiccate the meaning of intervention entirely; an intervention is never a deferral to act, but a decisive intercession.

The separation of videographers from the event is made stark by those who were decisively present. When camera-operators formed a perimeter around the incident to document, watch, and observe, they separated themselves from a present event. Though they spoke to the officers, their relationship to the event was like that of the distant viewers of their footage. The event itself was played out on the body of Rivera-Pitre. The de-arresters physically came between the NYPD officers and Rivera-Pitre, while the bystanders demonstrated the non-action of documentation.

As discussed above, documenters observe and record police with the expectation of efficacy, that some effect is made possible or likely by virtue of monitoring the police. Documenters rely on a response by viewers. For citizens concerned about those most chronically surveilled and policed, recording their routine encounters with officers may be influenced by a hope for solidarity. Certainly, this is not without cause. Media events have contributed to the growth of attention to incidents of police violence. That said, mass movements have emerged from undocumented incidents as well. For instance, in 2013, New York Police Department officers shot and killed a 16-year-old Black youth, named Kimani Gray. In 2014, Ferguson Police Officer Darren Wilson shot an 18-year old Black man, named Michael Brown. Neither of these incidents were filmed, and yet both produced mass mobilizations in the cities in which they occurred, and actions in solidarity elsewhere in the country. In fact, these two responses are among the largest and most sustained public reactions to police violence in the past decade. There is no certainty that the presence of video will aid the creation or building of political movements, nor is there certainty that an absence of video will hamper such developments.

One could reasonably claim the same about employment discipline and criminal prosecution of police officers who use unnecessary or excessive force. In the past decade, police have killed thousands of Americans, and yet only 54 police have been criminally charged for the killings (Kindy and Kelly). With such small numbers, it is difficult to make any certain assertions about the causal role played by video. Among those without video are cases like former Dallas Police Department Officer Bryan Burgess who in 2013 drove his police cruiser into a 51-year-old Black man, Fred Bradford, causing injuries from which Bradford later died. Despite an absence of video evidence, Burgess was fired and indicted for manslaughter.

Documentation proliferates not because of evidence of its efficacy in protecting people from excessive and unnecessary violence by police, but because it satisfies a normative prescription that has succeeded despite evidence of weak efficacy. People monitor police using camera phones because they receive all sorts of messages that confirm this transforms them from bystanders to interveners. The example of Rivera-Pitre throws this conflation of documentation and intervention into sharp relief. Video recording and shaming officers did not deter or de-escalate the violence against Rivera-Pitre; rather, it was the physical intervention of other protesters who de-arrested him that disrupted the violence of police.

1. Brucato advocates for increased video documentation of the public's interactions with police, citing not only issues that gave rise to the Black Lives Matter movement, but also reported incidents involving the Occupy Wall Street protests. Do you agree with this call to action? Why or why not?

2. The article suggests that there may have been repercussions for those who filmed some of the events referenced. Do you agree with this assertion? If you were writing a rebuttal, what reasons would you give to deny this allegation?

CHAPTER 5

WHAT THE MEDIA SAY

The media has not been shy in addressing the issue of police accountability. In the age of the internet, where the number of views is paramount in driving revenue, videos of police interactions with suspects—including graphic videos of shootings or use of force—have been prevalent, driving much of the conversation in comment sections as well as spilling out onto social media.

In the first selection of this chapter, Matthew Standerfer notes another court decision on how and when suspects can be frisked in a piece for *Cronkite News*. Then, Waging Non-Violence takes a short look at historical interactions with police, including the origination of the term "police brutality" and suggests some alternatives to relying on police for dealing with community issues. Finally, journalist Elizabeth S. Hansen bridges the gap between an Arizona police force and the local community through her piece on a new community policing initiative.

"COURT REVERSES DRUG CONVICTION OVER FAULTY FRISK; DISSENT CALLS RULING 'DANGEROUS'," BY MATTHEW STANDERFER, FROM *CRONKITE NEWS*, NOVEMBER 28, 2012

WASHINGTON — A federal appeals court overturned a juvenile's felony drug conviction Wednesday, ruling that a Border Patrol pat-down that turned up marijuana during a vehicle stop in Arizona was not justified.

Writing for a split three-judge panel of the 9th U.S. Circuit Court of Appeals, Judge N.R. Smith said the frisk "exceeded the scope of a constitutional ... search," which requires a reasonable belief that a suspect poses a threat to officers.

But in a scathing dissent, Judge Alex Kozinski said the majority opinion in the case of the juvenile, identified only as I.E.V., was "wrong" and "dangerous."

"Any officer who sent I.E.V. on his way without finding out what he was hiding under his shirt should have been fired for incompetence," Kozinski wrote.

The juvenile was riding in a vehicle driven by his brother, Joseph Mendez, when they entered a Border Patrol checkpoint near Whetstone, Ariz., about 100 miles from the Mexican border. After a police dog signaled the possible presence of people or drugs hidden in the vehicle, officers had the two get out of the car.

At that point, the dog gave no indication that the two had contraband on them. When Mendez consented to a search of the vehicle, nothing turned up.

One officer frisked Mendez and found no contraband, but when another officer frisked I.E.V. he felt a lump and lifted the youth's shirt to find a "brick" of marijuana taped to his abdomen. That sparked a second pat-down of Mendez, uncovering more drugs.

The arrest report mentioned "nervous behavior and gestures of Mendez," but not of I.E.V. They both cooperated.

Smith wrote that this was not a situation where the officers could reasonably have believed they were in danger, which might have justified frisks. He pointed to testimony that officers did not find the passengers to be threatening, in possession of an observable weapon or attempting to flee.

"The officers largely completed their investigatory tasks before frisking Mendez, the fidgety one," Smith wrote.

"Though we take no satisfaction in the consequence that a possessor of marijuana will escape punishment in this case, our overriding concern is that to hold otherwise would allow police officers to frisk every individual in a vehicle stopped based on reasonable suspicion of criminal activity," he wrote.

Kozinski agreed that frisking is an "indignity and intrusion" but that it needs to be balanced against the safety of the officers.

"It's easy enough ... to say that officers in the field had no cause to fear for their safety," he wrote. "But if we'd been there ... and seen one of the suspects fidget like he was reaching for a weapon, I'd have dived for cover into the nearest ditch, and my guess is I wouldn't have been the first one there."

I.E.V.'s attorney, John Kaufmann, said the judges wanted to spell out what the law is on stop-and-frisk.

"The important thing to remember is this was less than a pound of marijuana," Kaufmann said.

"The juvenile got the aggravated felony of possession of marijuana with intent to distribute," he said.

"The brother was given a misdemeanor. I don't think the appellate court thought that was right."

Kaufmann said I.E.V. has served more time than Mendez, and regardless of the final court outcome, his punishment is already over.

A Justice Department spokesman declined to comment on the ruling.

1. This article appears on the surface to be very non-biased. What quotes did the writer pull from the decision (and the dissent) that may reveal the writer's opinion on this issue? How do you think those quotes may sway readers?

2. This decision relates back to the issue of the Terry stop, in which suspects stopped for one alleged issue can be searched for other issues. Does this decision change your opinion of Terry stops? Why or why not?

"WHAT IS TO BE DONE ABOUT POLICE BRUTALITY IN THE AGE OF THE NEW JIM CROW?" BY MARIAM ELBA, FROM WAGING NON-VIOLENCE, JULY 8, 2014

Whether officers are pepper-spraying protesters in the face or shooting and killing people in the back while in custody, police forces throughout the United States continue to have a reputation for being institutions that abuse their power. Last week, in yet another instance of police brutality, a California Highway Patrol officer was filmed beating a 51-year-old Marlene Pinnock to the ground. The Pinnock family has stated that they plan to take legal action and file a lawsuit against the California Highway Patrol.

This is just one among thousands of such incidents that happen yearly in the United States. Among the most notable incidents in recent years were the shootings of 22-year-old Oakland resident Oscar Grant in 2008 — while in police custody — and Brooklyn teenager Kimani Gray in 2013. Both cases elevated the issue of racist policing to the forefront of the national dialogue.

Police brutality has a long history in the United States, especially police violence targeting people of color. Interestingly, the usage of the term "police brutality" began at the turn of the 20th century with the beginning of the Prohibition Era and the exponential increase in crime. Brutality has been used as a state tactic to suppress social movements from the Civil Rights movement to anti-war protests during the Vietnam War, and as a tool to maintain the racial caste system that many are calling the New Jim Crow, which is aided by the so-called War on Drugs.

Organized resistance to police violence by groups like the Black Panther Party in the 1960s to contemporary organizing like the Safe Outside the System Project have sought to create alternatives to policing in black and brown communities throughout the country. Grassroots organizations such as Communities United for Police Reform, CopWatch and CopBlock have not only been providing updates on the latest incidents of police violence, but also helping victims take legal action. For example, CopWatch has distributed a guide detailing what to do if one is held unjustly in police custody. These organizations provide handy resources and advice on what to do when stopped by the police, such as the protocol to always write down the officers' names and badge numbers if you feel you are being mistreated.

With Pinnock's case hanging in the balance, continuing to film, document and share these instances of police violence will help the movement gain awareness and more support from different sectors.

1. The writer here references historical as well as current anti-violence and self-policing groups. Do you think these groups can replace police in communities that have faced conflict with police departments? Why or why not?

2. The article references the origination of the term "police brutality" as being during the Prohibition Era. What do you think may have led to this change in how the police were perceived during this era and why?

"POLICE AND CITIZENS TO UNITE IN COMMUNITY OUTREACH PROGRAM," BY ELIZABETH S. HANSEN, FROM *CRONKITE NEWS*, AUGUST 11, 2016

MESA — When Susan Monroe, then a 32-year-old single mother, considered applying for a deputy position with the Maricopa County Sheriff's Office, she spoke with her children about the risks.

"The one thing [my son] asked me was 'What if you get shot?'" she said. "And I told him … it's part of my job … one of those things that I may have to put myself between the good guy and the bad guy, or even between two bad guys."

It's a personal risk Monroe said officers take every day on the job to protect their communities, and she said it is one that members of the community might not truly understand.

Now, about 12 years after she went through the police academy, Monroe is participating in a new program called Police and Community Working Together to try to establish more personal relationships and understanding between individual deputies and families in the community.

The PACT program is a collaboration between the Maricopa County Sheriff's Office, the Mesa Police Department and the Mesa Dr. Martin Luther King Celebration Committee, an organization that focuses on promoting peace and equality.

MCSO has four deputies who will participate in the PACT program, according to Paul Chagolla, deputy chief and bureau commander for the Maricopa County Sheriff's Office Support Services Bureau One and Community Outreach department. Assistant Chief Michael Soelberg of the Mesa Police Department said four to six of his officers are also expected to participate in the program.

Each officer will be paired with a family from the community for a month. Each week, the officer will spend up to three hours doing activities with that family, such as game nights or having dinner together. The participants will be able to submit suggestions for activities, and Angela Booker, 52, president of the Mesa MLK Committee, said

Mesa MLK board members will decide which to approve to ensure the families and officers are comfortable with the suggested activity.

"In the MLK board, we were trying to figure out what we can do to help the community," Booker said. "Where I grew up, we knew the police … we had a close community. And that's what we need now."

"When we developed the community outreach team," Chagolla said, "it started with this idea of we wanted to show the community what we see in ourselves."

DEEPER ISSUES

While the Mesa Dr. Martin Luther King Celebration Committee seeks to use the PACT program to improve communication, negotiations to get the program going illustrate just how challenging that can be.

Formal meetings between officers and families have been delayed for almost a year, as the Mesa MLK board has been trying to work out language for program materials.

When Booker presented the PACT program to the Mesa Police Department, officers wanted Mesa MLK to change wording in materials about officer-involved shootings.

"They didn't like us saying the number of people being killed [by officers]," Booker said. "They wanted us to narrow it down and say how many people were killed who were doing something illegal, how many people who were killed were just like in a police stop. And how many people who were killed that they're still working on the cases."

Soelberg said the language presented law enforcement in a negative light.

"When you talk about shootings, the officers can take offense to it. When you talk about murdering people," Soelberg said, "obviously, there's deadly use of force encounters, but those are use of force encounters that are unfortunate when they happen."

"That's why we took a little break to say, 'Let's reassess this. Let's get some verbiage in there that it's agreeable to both sides,'" he added.

Data about officer-involved shootings comes from many different sources.

According to a database created by The Washington Post, 990 people were "shot dead" by police in 2015, 42 of whom were in Arizona.

According to FBI data, 41 law enforcement officers were feloniously killed in the line of duty in the same year (2015) nationwide. The most recent data for Arizona states that three officers were "feloniously killed" in 2014.

In addition, the Gun Violence Archive data shows there were 79 officer-involved shootings in 2015 in Arizona. Forty of those incidents resulted in at least one death. Some of the incidents involved someone shot while engaged in a criminal activity. In many cases in the archive, information about specific circumstances is not available.

After months of delays, the PACT program is currently set to start this month with MCSO, and the Mesa Police Department is set to join at the end of this month or in early September.

Mesa MLK hopes to use donations and grants to cover the cost of the activities.

"We don't want to put burden on the officer or the family to pay for it," Booker said.

Chagolla said in an email that, while officers can volunteer in the program, they could receive compensation depending on the types of activities they complete.

Some officers and families have already met informally at some events, including a community forum.

Booker said Mesa MLK does not know of any programs like PACT, and the group wants more volunteers to apply for the program and to eventually take it nationwide.

Soelberg said he and his team hope that the program participants can take what they learn and get others involved with this or other programs to further a relationship between police and the community.

"That's just at the core of building that relationship: getting people involved," Soelberg said. "Letting [civilians] know what to do and not to do, when to call, who to call when you need help."

In addition to the PACT program, Monroe works with MCSO on other community projects, such as reading to children and giving books to teenage mothers to read to their children. According to Monroe and MCSO, reaching out to families and young people helps decrease their chances of being in the criminal justice system in the first place.

She added that even though they only work with one or two people at a time with community-interaction programs such as these, "you've got to start somewhere."

DIFFERENT CULTURES

One of the PACT goals is to help the officers and the participants, as well as others in the community, understand each other and appreciate how much they have in common.

To further an understanding, the program participants will be given questions to facilitate a conversation.

They will write about their experiences in a journal to share at group meetings.

Booker said that, for some members of the community, especially people of color, being pulled over by a police officer can bring up many painful memories.

For her husband, she said it brings to mind childhood memories.

"At recess time, they played dodge ball," Booker said, "and they would put him in the center and he was always the one they threw the balls at [because of his race]."

"When you're coming up in an environment like that, and it's constantly every day in your face, we want police to know all of that is inside of us," she said.

That's why she might get a little antsy or upset when an officer pulls up to her.

"It's all those little steps from a child to being an adult," she said.

Since Booker moved to Arizona in 2011, she said she's been stopped four times by police officers.

"We had a policeman run our plates, follow us to our subdivision, and make sure that we actually lived there," she said. "He waited until the garage door went up, then he sat there for a couple of minutes just to make sure it was our house."

Ladina Willis, a 54-year-old volunteer board member with the Mesa MLK Celebration Committee, said you don't always know the mindset of the civilian being pulled over.

"What if they just lost all their family members?" she said. "You never know the situation."

Willis said she knows there's an issue.

"I think that in part, for me, that you got to work on how to interact with different cultures and people," Willis said.

She added that her daughter, who's biracial and looks white, has been affected by the shootings of officers in Dallas and the high-profile shootings of unarmed black men across the country, and she has written about it on a blog.

"She said, 'I never thought that I would say this, but it's almost like you feel safe that your skin is white,'" Willis said. "And she was sad that she had to say that."

Soelberg said his team wants to develop a relationship with both those who support the police department and those who have more negative perceptions of officers.

"We're open to listening to everybody on both positive and negative," he said, "because we have to build the relationships with both sides."

Monroe echoed the idea of understanding others.

"I think there's a lot of people that don't wish any ill will on law enforcement, but I think there are some that are just angry at the system and angry at government overall," Monroe said.

"We see people on the worst day of their life for the most part," she said, starting to choke up. "When you're holding that baby in your hands that dies, when you respond to a call from a child that got basically their head bit off by the family dog just by sitting and playing."

Monroe said those are the kinds of experiences that many people in the community do not understand.

Another MCSO deputy, 38-year-old Hector Martinez, said officers must remember that the community is not all bad.

"We have to keep in mind...not [to] have that cop mentality that a lot of police officers have," Martinez said, "the mentality of us versus them."

"I think that's where we need to start changing … stop looking at everybody as being something different," Monroe said. "I look at it as everybody has something unique to offer."

"We're all the same," she added. "We all bleed red."

1. The article notes that this program was delayed due to language issues. What types of language do you think the police disagreed with? How do you think the ending language may have looked in the final documentation?

2. Booker notes that prior experience may affect how people of color react during a police stop. What information would you suggest police officers have in mind during police stops involving people of color? How do you think that might affect the outcomes of stops?

CHAPTER 6

WHAT ORDINARY PEOPLE SAY

Naturally, a topic as controversial as police brutality attracts the attention of average citizens, many of whom form opinions based on the media coverage as noted in the previous chapter. Here we'll look at what some of these ordinary citizens have to say about police-related issues.

In "Race + Class = What "Police Brutality" Means for Some (But Definitely, Not All) Black Folks," Honorée Fanonne Jeffers discusses the matter of economic status and how that may impact how citizens, especially those of color, interact with police forces in the US. Is it possible that a change of economic circumstances can lead to a difference in incidents involving police?

Next, Jason Hughey looks at the aftermath of rioting and looting in Baltimore and the impact faced by the city after the Freddie Gray protests in "What's Next for Baltimore?"

And finally, Brett Dickerson examines how
police have been interacting with citizens, and
through his personal conversations with a retired
police chief, how the public's relationship with the
police has changed over time in "Police Cannot Be
an Occupying Army in a Democracy."

"RACE + CLASS = WHAT 'POLICE BRUTALITY' MEANS FOR SOME (BUT DEFINITELY, NOT ALL) BLACK FOLKS," BY HONORÉE FANONNE JEFFERS, FROM *PHILLIS REMASTERED*, AUGUST 26, 2014

I just don't write super quickly about emotionally charged
events anymore, because when I do, usually I say something stupid and hurt somebody's feelings without meaning
to. And it took me having a really deep, teary conversation
with a dear friend last night (over something that didn't
even start out being about police brutality) to collect my
thoughts.

So here goes.

I don't want to dismiss anyone's grief over the killing
of the child Mike Brown—yes, child; when you get to be my
age, you understand just how young eighteen is. And yes, I'm
sad, too. Just because I don't talk about my grief in a way that
makes people feel comfortable doesn't mean I don't have it.

But I also have had some anger. And that anger is
over class.

And when I say "class," I'm not talking about those
silly, obvious, and rather useless "class" markers, such
as whether somebody has walked around with his pants
hanging down, or whether somebody has previously been
arrested, or whether somebody was "asking for it."

And when I say anger, I'm not just talking about anger over racism—which is sticky thing to catch ahold of. I'm talking about how no one really wants to address that the lived experiences of contemporary, college-educated, middle-class, black people and the lived experiences of contemporary, formally-uneducated, poor, black people are vastly different when it comes to racialized violence at the hands of the police.

I'm not the first person who has talked about race and class, and I won't be the last person. And I'm not the first person who has talked about violence at the hands of the police is class-based, either. But I have been searching for someone who really understands that race plus class is a very real, existing intersectionality that some black folks–even so-called "correct" black folks–don't "get" or experience in the least.

Oh, lately, there's so much talk about "racism in America" and what it means. So much talk about whether white folks without black friends are racist, when, let's face it, *I'm* pretty choosy about my black friends. I'm pretty choosy about my white friends. I'm just choosy like that. But should I now run out and get me some more to prove something to somebody?

But let's also face that there is a difference between the issues confronted by middle-class black people who want to be liked, accepted, and assimilated into mainstream (i.e. white) culture and who feel diminished by that culture versus the issues of life or death confronted by the bodies and psyches of poor black people in overwhelmingly segregated neighborhoods that are policed by white police officers.

Because, look, don't no white cop shoot an unarmed black child to death because said white cop don't think

Lupita is cute and/or he ain't got nobody black to go to the Applebee's with Sunday after church. This goes deeper than just "race", and this goes deeper than some ephemeral talk about "this is what slavery was like."

Sidebar: And as a student of history, I really wish that folks who are not real students of history–or who have never been slaves– would stop thinking they know about slavery simply because they retweet something on Twitter. Try reading an actual history book or three hundred. Okay? I just needed to say that.

Let us return.

When we think about the direct line of descent from the plantation overseer—a working class white man—and the slave patrollers—made up of "Yeoman" farmers or other working class white men—down to most southern, white police forces now, we need to consider that contemporary police forces in the south are over-whelmingly populated with working class white men.

And what do the overseer, the slave patrollers, and contemporary southern police forces have in common? They traditionally have been used for the past three hundred years or so years to keep poor black folks "in line."

By the way, I've read a history book or three hundred. Just so you know.

These southern, overwhelmingly white police forces impact young black people from poor neighbor-hoods on a daily basis. We are talking about the terrifying onslaught on poor, black neighborhoods in which the police are used to keep poor black people "in line"—and in their own "quarters."

Yes, middle class black people have experienced racism, but we might call the first level of this racism "racial insult." (And these are just my own categories.)

Racial insults might entail being followed in a store or being talked to in a disrespectful, cruel manner by white coworkers or student colleagues. Maybe you stood in line at the Piggly Wiggly and the clerk pretended you weren't next. That kind of racism takes a toll on your psyche—trust, I know—but it does not propel six bullets through your body and brain.

Then, there's the next level of racism: we might call those instances "racial harassment."

Racial harassment entails the time or two that one middle-class young black man was stopped and harassed by the police. He might have even been arrested, pushed onto the hood of the car, roughed up and made to fear for his life. But at the end of it all, he was able to call his parents, a mentor, or reach into his wallet and pull out the business card upon which his attorney's name has been embossed.—I am not dismissing the experience of that black man, but what I am saying is, there is a difference between a kid whose parents can bail him out of jail and a kid whose parents have to call a bail bondsman.

And then, we have the third, highest level of racism: "racial violence." This is where a black person is injured and/or killed by someone in a hate-based crime.

And you might say now, "But, Honorée, we know *your* background. So who are *you* to bring this up? And are *you* seriously trying to say that you know the difference, with your bourgie, middle-class, professor self?"

But yet, I do know the difference, very distinctly. Because yes, I've been poor, and yes, I've been middle-class and yes, I've seen—though not experienced— all three levels of racism first hand. Surprise.

When my parents separated, we suddenly became poor. My mother, sister, and I lived in what was then called

"Section-8 housing" in Southwest DeKalb County, Georgia, and then, in a "poor" black neighborhood in Atlanta. When we visited older relatives in the country (Eatonton) who were living on fixed incomes, they would give us their commodity foods: that huge loaf of so-called "cheese"— which, somehow made the most delicious grilled cheese sandwiches—and the other, processed food products upon which the names were brandished in bold letters: "Milk", "Peanut Butter," and so forth.

We ate meat only on the weekends, a lot of pinto beans and cornbread, and sweetened iced tea which took away our appetite, though I don't think my mama was considering that at the time. And we lived with whole congregations of roaches and rats, sometimes at the same moments, some-times, at different intervals. And coming from my privileged, middle-class background of Durham, North Carolina, I was extremely demoralized by my poverty—but I soon under-stood, so were other black kids who did not come from where I came from.

Example: we had the "free" or reduced" stamped on our lunch tickets, and the sticker was very prominent; the kids who didn't eat those lunches were aware of our financial state and sometimes made not-so-nice comments. And let me tell you, I was terrified that whoever had given my tasteful, carefully chosen outfits to the Goodwill might come upon me wearing them and call me out. My mother worked two jobs in addition to teaching and attending grad-uate school to keep my sister and me in pocket money so we could perpetrate like we weren't poor–sometimes leading to bills not being paid–but we never brought our "friends" from school over to visit.

This lasted only four years, but the memory of poverty is as fresh as it was over thirty years ago. The only thing that saved us was that my father died. My Columbia-educated, stingy, college professor-father who, bewilderingly, had taken out a prominent life insurance policy and named my mother as the sole beneficiary. After I left my poverty behind, I knew how lucky I was. The other kids that had that stamp on their lunch card did not have the same background as I, a background which I moved into the foreground with stunningly relieved and brisk grace.

Yes, this is my "class confession." There are many, many things you do not know about me.

I think about those kids sometimes. About those funky neighborhoods I lived in, where the white police were constantly patrolling, and where the black kids would say to me, "When they come up on you, don't run. If you run, they gone shoot."

At least once a month—thirty years later, as I sit in my cute, three-bedroom, two-bathroom house in my white neighborhood—I think about my "cut-buddy" friends, Black and Junior and Scut. I think about whether they made it out of their twenties alive. And when I made it to graduate school, I promised myself, I would do anything to never be poor again. Anything.

And I did do anything. I sucked up to white folks to get ahead in my career, I put away my "race rage," I learned how, when I moved my speech into the black vernacular to laughingly remind people that I was "code switching"–lest, as a (former) white friend told me once, I came off sounding ignorant– and here I am, middle-class again. I can admit the self-effacing, sometimes humiliating actions that kept my thing intact.

We talk about race of our "white allies" and "white privilege" when we talk about the fight against racism. But at some point, I would like us to think of the *class* of middle class "black allies" who do not have the same experiences that poor black people go through every day.

What are the roles of the middle-class black people who, once the dust has cleared from the protests of Ferguson, Missouri and a child's funeral is over, can once again fly back home on tickets purchased with their credit cards, and then, walk through their much "nicer," safe neighborhoods, and drive their late-model vehicles into the two-car garage attached to a home bought with credit based upon jobs at places of business (or education) where they are surrounded by white people they must get along with—and all without the daily fear of the assault on their actual bodies, but only, an assault to their feelings or senses of self-esteem?

I think a lot about the issues I've mentioned in this post. I'm asking you to do the same. And after you think, even if you decide you don't agree with me, just because we don't agree doesn't mean I'm not sad a black child is dead.

1. The author of this post references division even among people of color when it comes to police interactions. Do you think she is correct in her statement that economic status plays a part in how citizens interact with police? Why or why not?

2. Assuming that the author's assertion is true, do you think this might also be true for white people? Use an example to back up your answer.

"WHAT'S NEXT FOR BALTIMORE?" BY JASON HUGHEY, FROM *DEBATE THE STATE*, APRIL 29, 2015

As I write this, the National Guard and local police are enforcing a curfew in Baltimore. The curfew began at 10 p.m. and will be lifted at 5 a.m.

We all know why there's a curfew, of course. We've seen the videos of buildings on fire, cars being smashed, and violent clashes with police. We've seen mobs tearing through the streets, ransacking and looting as they go. We've read about the reporters who had their faces smashed in by rioting thugs. We've watched a mother berate and smack her son for taking part in the madness.

We all know how it started too. We know Freddie Gray's name and we know he died after his spinal cord was 80% severed at the neck while he was being arrested by Baltimore police officers.

Tonight, as law enforcement officials patrol the streets of Baltimore, many hope that some semblance of order will be restored to the city. Some will look to the picture of a young black boy handing out water bottles to the police and see hope for restoration. Others will praise the courage of a Vietnam veteran named Robert Valentine for standing up to the rioters and telling them to go home. Many will pray for the innocent victims who were caught in the crossfire.

But no matter what, all of us will have a difficult time comprehending the meaning of what we just saw. The road ahead for Baltimore, and for all of us who seek to hold the police accountable for brutality, is going to be filled with the debris of burned down buildings and busted cars. There will be anger. There will be political posturing. There will be

high-strung emotions. Consequently, it will be crucial in
the coming days and weeks to understand Baltimore's
nightmare from a calm and level-headed perspective. It
will be essential for us to know what is true and proceed
from that basis.

Thus, here is what we know is true about Baltimore:

1. **The city of Baltimore has a rampant and undeniable
   problem with police brutality.** For years, Baltimore's
   citizens, especially minorities, have felt the heavy hand
   of a corrupt police force. Between 2011 and 2014 alone,
   the city was forced to pay out $5.7 million to victims of
   police brutality. Given the scope of violence detailed in
   Conor Friedersdorf's article, there's no way to merely
   excuse Baltimore's police violence problem as a result
   of a handful of bad apples on the force. The problem is
   systemic. Freddie Gray's death was merely the straw
   that broke the camel's back and sparked a long over-
   due outrage.

2. **Experiencing deep anger, mortification, and sadness
   over Freddie Gray's death is more than justified.** In fact,
   people should feel these emotions when considering
   the recent history of policing in Baltimore, not just in
   contemplating Gray's case. If you had the chance to
   read my letter to Franklin Graham, you'll know that I've
   experienced these emotions when researching cases
   of police brutality all over the country. Righteous indig-
   nation is a healthy response to such abuses of authority.

3. **Peaceful protesting is a legitimate way to express frus-
   tration with modern policing while honoring victims
   of police brutality.** Granted, its effectiveness at solving
   the problem of police abuse is likely to be minimal at

best, but at least it's a healthy way to process one's emotions. In Baltimore, peaceful protests preceded the rioting and as the dust is settling more peaceful protestors are re-emerging. A lot of citizens are helping to clean up the city in the midst of conducting their protests. These people are expressing their sympathy for Gray and their anger over his death in a proper way.

4. **Regardless of one's motivation, destruction of private property and injury of innocent life is completely unjustified. No excuses, no exceptions.** The rioters who wantonly destroyed private property, looted businesses, and injured a number of innocent people were engaging in activities just as evil as any clear-cut case of police brutality. Just ask the reporters who experienced the mob's wrath firsthand. Unfortunately, there are some people who will excuse the actions of the rioters on the basis of their cause or out of anger toward police brutality. That reaction is completely and totally wrong—it promotes exactly the same sort of behavior that we oppose when we decry police brutality. We must condone no one, whether they are wearing a badge or not, in violating another individual's rights to life and property.

5. **Opponents of systemic police brutality are not akin to the violent rioters in Baltimore, nor is it possible to accuse them of supporting such violence.** If you doubt this, see points #2, #3, and #4. Unfortunately, the Baltimore rioters just made the job of those who decry police abuse much harder by turning the national spotlight towards their looting and away from the systemic problem of police violence. However, many who

oppose modern policing tactics also condemn the rioters in Baltimore. Therefore, it is intellectually dishonest
to accuse all critics of modern policing of encouraging
the violence in Baltimore (or Ferguson for that matter).

Ultimately, the issue of police brutality must not be
overlooked as Baltimore attempts to recover from the events
of the past few days. I wish that Freddie Gray was only one of
a handful of cases to discuss, but he's not. In Baltimore alone,
there's more problems with police brutality than should ever
be allowed to happen in a country that calls itself the "land
of the free." The wrong actions of a few looters must not be
allowed to drown out the needed conversation for addressing
widespread abuses at the hands of police officers.

Likewise, simplistic accusations that portray all cops
as being racist, badge-wearing thugs will be unhelpful. The
same can be said for expressions of undying affection for
the Heroes of the Blue Shield. The problem is not that all
cops are racist and the solution is not to worship the idea of
the police. The problem is that systemic abuses of authority
result in far too many Freddie Gray's and the solution is—well,
that's another article for another time.

Tomorrow, Baltimore's citizens will face a new day.
Whether the unrest is fully under control remains to be
seen. But regardless of whether or not tonight's curfew
effectively restores order, the most important questions
posed by the crisis in Baltimore will likely remain unan-
swered for weeks to come. As we try to come to grips with
the events of the past week, one simple fact remains: yet
another tragic chapter in our national conversation on
police abuse has been written.

I hope that someday we will be able to write
the epilogue.

1. Hughey claims that peaceful protests' "effectiveness at solving the problem of police abuse is likely to be minimal at best." Do you think that history supports this claim? Why or why not?

2. Rioting and looting impacts more than just the police force. What other parts of a community are affected by these acts? Do you think that helps or hurts a cause overall? Why or why not?

"POLICE CANNOT BE AN OCCUPYING ARMY IN A DEMOCRACY," BY BRETT DICKERSON, FROM *BRETT DICKERSON – JOURNALIST*, AUGUST 14, 2014

It's clear by now that the situation in Ferguson, Missouri, went way too far. How do we have local police dressing up in hardened riot gear and using military-style weapons as well as military-style vehicles? How is it considered wise to *start* with that response at the first sign of trouble?

It hasn't always been that way. There are great examples of effective policing that allows for free speech and assembly and protects those rights.

CITIZENS AGREE TO BE POLICED IF THERE IS TRUST

Before his death, retired Oklahoma City Police Chief Wayne Lawson used to talk to me about his experiences in law enforcement.* The most striking thing about all of his stories were that they were about how a citizen had helped him out just when he was about to get hurt or killed.

But when I found out his work history, it made perfect sense. The first assignment that he had as a young officer was walking a beat—a foot patrol—in the tough Capital Hill area of Oklahoma City. But it wasn't like in the movies. He walked that beat by himself. And the only communication with the central station was at an occasional call box. No radios. Those came much later.

It was on that beat that he learned how critical it was for him to make every friend that he legitimately could. The police are almost always outnumbered, but when walking a foot patrol by yourself, that is radically true.

In that environment he learned that his ability to police that population had everything to do with his knowledge of them, their knowledge of him as a fair and honest cop, and his ability to make friends. The gun he carried was important to his safety, but not in any way important to his ability to police the population. *They agreed for him to police them.*

VIOLENCE AVERTED IN THE TURBULENT '60S

Years later, in 1969, as Police Chief, he helped avoid what easily could have turned into the worse riot in the history of the city. But it was averted with not so much as a bloody nose because of his knowledge of all the people of the city, including its black population. It was also due to his respect for the population's need and right to free speech and assembly.

The event was the "Black Friday" protest that was planned because of the city's response to protests by the garbage workers, most of whom were black. They had gone on strike earlier in the week and a series of declarations and threats had been issued earlier by the mayor while he was also reaching out to the leaders of the black citizens.

The day came. A large protest march happened that ended at City Hall. Expressions of disappointment with the City Council and Mayor were expressed. Lawson stood right next to the protest leaders on the steps of City Hall and provided the bull horn for them to speak to the crowd.

According to a couple of stories from that day, it turned out to be positive from many angles.

Originally, protesters were not going to be allowed to approach City Hall. But at the last minute, Lawson's gut told him that there would be a better way to handle the emotions of the moment.

At the end of the speeches, Lawson addressed the crowd in a way that seems strange in this day of tough-guy posturing from the Police Chief and police of Ferguson:

There was no violence then or later as other protests took place around the city in following days. Why? It was tremendous leadership and hard work by black community leaders who insisted on peaceful protest. Without their work, events could have taken a very negative turn.

Also, it was due to Lawson's knowledge of the people who he was policing. I also knew one of his majors from that time, and he had the same sharp knowledge of people in general and the sub-cultures of Oklahoma City in specific. Lawson demanded that from his leaders and officers.

He was a contemporary of infamous police chiefs of the 1960s such as Rocky Pomerance of Miami Beach, Florida, and Bull Connor of Birmingham, Alabama. But his approach to law enforcement, especially during the hard times of large, angry protests was deeply different.

And that's what is important to the current distressing
situation in Ferguson, Missouri.

POLICE HAVE CHOICES

The police leaders there *do have a choice* about how they
will respond to these protests. And now, their responses
show little regard for the people who depend upon the
police for their safety and well-being. Except in this case,
the police are a cause for fear, not only from the black
citizens of Ferguson, but from reporters who are trying to
cover the events happening there.

Starting this situation with riot gear, military-style
weapons/vehicles, and threats was not the way to diffuse
an already tense situation that had been caused in the
first place by aggressive, antagonistic policing that lead
to a citizen's death. There is a difference in how police
and city leaders chose to respond to difficult situations.

The response of the mostly white police department
controlled by a mostly white city council in a city that is
over 60% black is more like an occupying army than a
police force. The change has to happen in Ferguson, but
there are many other communities where a remote and
overly aggressive police department have created smol-
dering resentments waiting to be touched off.

Ferguson can be a way for us to have this conversation about what is effective policing and how it is different
from a military occupation of a hostile population.

**But it starts with relief for the citizens of Ferguson.
It's time for the rest of us — citizens of the entire nation —
to demand better choices that respect the Constitutional
protections that citizens and the press have been given.**

* My relationship to Wayne Lawson was my good fortune due to my being assigned as pastor to the church that he and his wife had been a member of for many years. They lived in Oklahoma City their entire adult lives. He was my parishioner until his death when I co-officiated his funeral with another pastor who had been a life-long friend.

1. Dickerson notes that there has to be an ongoing trust between the public and the police for a democracy to succeed. Do you agree with his belief that this trust relationship has eroded over time? If so, how could that be remedied? If not, what examples do you see of trust between police and communities?

2. This article notes an issue that comes up in discussing police issues: how similar police are armed in comparison to our military. Do you feel this is the best way for police to continue providing public safety? What changes would you make, if any, in what tools police use in interactions with the public?

CONCLUSION

Hopefully by now you have a new understanding of police actions in the United States and a new perspective on the issues facing police, legislators, the courts, and the activists who are working for change in how the police interact with the communities they serve. As with all social changes, there is often unrest and disagreement on both sides of an issue before any long-lasting social changes come about.

Many view the current climate regarding police as a second Civil Rights Movement, with much of the underlying structures of our criminal justice system still tied into the same social constructs that people of color were fighting in the 1960s. There are others who view those who protest policing practices to be criminals: a refusal to obey the laws of the country they live in.

We've examined both sides of the issue through various articles and court decisions, but some questions remain. Did you have an opinion before you read this book? If so, did it change at all based on what you read? Did you gain anything from reading about the other side of the issue?

If you had no opinion, do you have one now?

The goal for any type of informed opinion is to read widely and across both sides of any issue to better understand what's at play as well as any historical background that may have an impact on either side. We hope that you've had the opportunity to sample a bit of that here, and will continue to critically evaluate the texts that you read. In an era where "fake news" is a buzzword, reading critically and empathetically across the divide is crucial to a functioning society.

BIBLIOGRAPHY

Bhugowandeen, Bela. "Diversity in the British Police: Adapting to a Multicultural Society." *Cahiers du MIMMOC*, 2013. https://mimmoc.revues.org/1340.

Brucato, Ben. "Standing By Police Violence: On the Constitution of the Ideal Citizen as Sousveiller." *American Studies Journal*, Number 61 (2016). http://www.asjournal.org/61-2016/standing-police-violence-constitution-ideal-citizen-sousveiller.

Buttar, Shahid and Sophia Cope. "Court's Decision on Recording Police Erodes First Amendment Rights and Transparency While Inviting Violence." Electronic Frontier Foundation, April 6, 2016. https://www.eff.org/deeplinks/2016/02/decision-eroding-first-amendments-rights-civil-rights-transparency-inviting-violence.

Dickerson, Brett. "Police Cannot Be An Occupying Army in a Democracy." *Brett Dickerson – Journalist*, August 14, 2014. http://www.brettdickerson.net/police-cannot-be-an-occupying-army-in-a-democracy.

Elba, Mariam. "What Is to Be Done About Police Brutality in the Age of the New Jim Crow?" Waging Non-Violence, July 8, 2014. http://wagingnonviolence.org/2014/07/done-police-brutality-age-new-jim-crow.

Fortenbery, Jay. "Improving Motivation and Productivity of Police Officers." *FBI Law Enforcement Bulletin*, 2015. https://leb.fbi.gov/2015/august/improving-motivation-and-productivity-of-police-officers.

Gowder, Paul. "A Small Sign of Hope on This Dark Day for the Movement for Black Lives." *Medium*, September 21, 2016. https://medium.com/@PaulGowder/a-small-sign-of-hope-on-this-dark-day-for-the-movement-for-black-lives-a998f3e2d2aa.

Hansen, Elizabeth S. "Police and Citizens to Unite in Community Outreach Program." *Cronkite News*, August 11, 2016. https://cronkitenews.azpbs.org/2016/08/11/police-community-come-together-pact.

Hughey, Jason. "What's Next for Baltimore?" *Debate the State*, April 29, 2015. http://www.debatethestate.com/2015/04/29/whats-next-for-baltimore.

Jeffers, Honorée Fanonne. "Race + Class = What "Police Brutality" Means for Some (But Definitely, Not All) Black Folks." *Phillis Remastered*, August 26, 2014. https://phillisremastered.com/2014/08/26/race-class-what-police-brutality-means-for-some-but-definitely-not-all-black-folks.

Joh, Elizabeth E. "*Maryland v. King*: "Three Concerns About Policing and Genetic Information." *Genomics Law Report:* A

Publication of the Law Firm Robinson Bradshaw & Hinson, September 19, 2013. http://www.genomicslawreport.com/index .php/2013/09/19/maryland-v-king-three-concerns-about -policing-and-genetic-information.

Kille, Leighton Walter. "Hot Spots Policing and Crime Prevention Strategies: Ongoing Research." *Journalist's Resource*, July 11, 2013. https://journalistsresource.org/studies/government /criminal-justice/hot-spot-policing-strategies.

Lynch, Alicia. "When Police Are Part of the Problem of Violence: The Case of Papua New Guinea's Police Force." Seeds Theatre Group Inc., October 8, 2014. http://www.seedstheatre .org/when-police-are-part-of-the-problem-the-case-of -papua-new-guineas-police-force.

McElvain, James P., Augustine J. Kposowa, and Brian C. Gray. "Testing a Crime Control Model: Does Strategic and Directed Deployment of Police Officers Lead to Lower Crime?" *Journal of Criminology*, Volume 2013, https://www.hindawi.com /archive/2013/980128.

Ortellado, Damian. "Emergency Room Reports Reveal Racial Disparity in Injuries Caused by Police." The Sunlight Foundation, September 4, 2014. https://sunlightfoundation .com/2014/09/04/cdc-hospital-reports-reveal-racial -disparity-in-injuries-caused-by-police.

Scarcini, Donald. "*Plumhoff v. Rickard*: When Is Police Use of Deadly Force Justified?" *Constitutional Law Reporter*, September 4, 2014. https://constitutionallawreporter.com/2014/09/04/ plumhoff-v-rickard-when-is-police-use-of-deadly-force-justi- fied.

Standerfer, Matthew. "Court Reverses Drug Conviction Over Faulty Frisk; Dissent Calls Ruling 'dangerous'." *Cronkite News*, November 28, 2013. http://cronkitenewsonline.com/2012/11 /court-reverses-drug-conviction-over-faulty-frisk-dissent -calls-ruling-dangerous/index.html.

US Commission on Civil Rights. "Revisiting *Who Is Guarding the Guardians?*" Retrieved April 5, 2016. http://www.usccr.gov/pubs /guard/exsum.htm.

US Supreme Court. *Kingsley v. Hendrickson.* June 22, 2015. https:// www.supremecourt.gov/opinions/14pdf/14-6368_m6hn.pdf.

Wihbey, John and Leighton Walter Kille. "Excessive or Reasonable Force by Police? Research on Law Enforcement and Racial Conflict." *Journalist's Resource*, July 18, 2016. https:// journalistsresource.org/studies/government/criminal-justice /police-reasonable-force-brutality-race-research-review -statistics.

CHAPTER NOTES

CHAPTER 1: WHAT ACADEMICS, EXPERTS, AND RESEARCHERS SAY

"TESTING A CRIME CONTROL MODEL: DOES STRATEGIC AND DIRECTED DEPLOYMENT OF POLICE OFFICERS LEAD TO LOWER CRIME?" BY JAMES P. MCELVAIN, AUGUSTINE J. KPOSOWA, AND BRIAN C. GRAY

1. W. F. Walsh and G. F. Vito, "The meaning of Compstat: analysis and response," *Journal of Contemporary Criminal Justice*, vol. 20, pp. 51–68, 2004.
2. S. J. Gaffigan, *Understanding Community Policing: A Framework For Action [Monograph]*, Bureau of Justice Assistance, Department of Justice, Office of Justice Programs, National Institute of Justice, Washington, DC, USA, 1994.
3. H. Goldstein, *Problem-Oriented Policing*, McGraw-Hill, New York, NY, USA, 1990.
4. P. McDonald, *Managing Police Operations: Implementing the NYPD Crime Control Model Using COMPSTAT*, Wadsworth Publishing, Belmont, Mass, USA, 2002.
5. B. J. Palombo, "History of the professionalization of law enforcement," in *Academic Professionalism in Law Enforcement*, *B*. J. Palombo, Ed., Chapter 2, pp. 25–72, Garland, New York, NY, USA, 1995.
6. J. H. Skolnick and J. J. Fyfe, *Above the Law: Police and the Excessive Use of Force*, The Free Press, New York, NY, USA, 1993.
7. W. J. Bratton and S. W. Malinowski, "Police performance management in practice: taking COMPSTAT to the next level," *Policing*, vol. 2, pp. 259–265, 2008.
8. J. S. Magers, "Compstat: a new paradigm for policing or a repudiation of community policing?" *Journal of Contemporary Criminal Justice*, vol. 20, pp. 70–79, 2004.
9. P. McDonald, "COP, COMSTAT, and the new professionalism: mutual support or counterproductivity," in *Critical Issues in Policing*, R. G. Dunham and G. D. Alpert, Eds., pp. 255–277, Prospect Heights, 2001.
10. D. Weisburd, S. D. Mastrofski, A. M. McNally, R. Greenspan, and J. J. Willis, "Reforming to preserve: compstat and strategic problem solving in American policing," *Criminology & Public Policy*, vol. 2, pp. 421–456, 2003.

11. S. Sadd and R. M. Grinc, *Implementation Challenges in Community Policing: Innovative Neighborhood- Oriented Policing in Eight Cities*, Department of Justice, Office of Justice Programs, National Institute of Justice, Washington, DC, USA, 1996.

12. W. J. Bratton, "Research: a practitioner's perspective, from the streets: keynote speech as delivered at the 2006 National Institute of Justice Conference on July 17, 2006," *Western Criminology Review*, vol. 7, no. 3, pp. 1–6, 2006.

13. G. L. Kelling and W. J. Bratton, "Declining crime rates: Insiders' views of the New York City story," *Journal of Criminal Law and Criminology*, vol. 88, no. 4, p. 1217, 1998.

14. R. Rosenfeld, R. Fornango, and E. Baumer, "Did ceasefire, Compstat, and exile reduce homicide?" *Criminology & Public Policy*, vol. 4, pp. 419–449, 2005.

15. W. J. Bratton, "Cutting crime and restoring order: what America can learn from New Yorks finest. Heritage lecture #573," The Heritage Foundation Leadership for America, 1996, http://www.heritage.org /research/crime/hl573.cfm.

16. G. L. Kelling, T. Pate, D. Dieckman, and C. E. Brown, *The Kansas City Preventive Patrol Experiment: A Summary Report*, Police Foundation, Washington, DC, USA, 2003.

17. J. J. Willis, S. D. Mastrofski, and D. Weisburd, "COMPSTAT and bureaucracy: a case study of challenges and opportunities for change," *Justice Quarterly*, vol. 21, no. 3, pp. 463–496, 2004.

18. G. F. Vito, W. F. Walsh, and J. Kunselman, "Compstat: the manager's perspective," *International Journal of Police Science & Management*, vol. 7, pp. 187–196, 2004. View at Google Scholar

19. M. Long, S. Hallam, and E. B. Silverman, "The Anglo-American measurement of police performance: compstat and best value," *British Journal of Community Justice*, vol. 3, pp. 45–59, 2005.

20. J. Shane, *Compstat Implementation*, FBI Law Enforcement Bulletin, 2004.

21. V. E. Henry, *The COMPSTAT Paradigm: Management Accountability in Policing, Business and the Public Sector*, Looseleaf Law Publications, Flushing, NY, USA, 2003.

22. L. E. Cohen and M. Felson, "Social change and crime rate trends: a routine activity approach," *American Sociological Review*, vol. 44, pp. 588–605, 1979.

23. D. Weisburd, L. A. Wyckoff, J. Ready, J. E. Eck, J. C. Hinkle, and F. Gajewski, "Does crime just move around the corner? A controlled study of spatial displacement and diffusion of crime control benefits," *Criminology*, vol. 44, no. 3, pp. 549–591, 2006.

24. G. E. P. Box and G. M. Jenkins, *Time Series Analysis Forecasting and Control*, Holden Day, Oakland, Calif, USA, 1976.

25. R. Yaffee, *Introduction to Time Series Analysis and Forecasting*, Academic Press, San Diego, Calif, USA, 2000.

26. R. McCleary, R. Hay, E. E. Merdinger, and D. McDowell, *Applied Time Series Analysis for the Social Sciences*, Sage, Thousand Oaks, Calif, USA, 1980.

27. P. J. Diggle, *Time Series: A Biostatistical Introduction*, Clarendon Press, London, UK, 1990.

28. SAS Institute, *SAS/ETS: The AUTOREG Procedure [Computer Software Version 9. 3]*, SAS Institute, Cary, NC, USA, 2010.

29. G. L. Kelling and W. H. Sousa, "Do police matter? An analysis of the impact of New York Citys Police reforms," *Manhattan Institute Civic Report*, 2001, http://www.manhattan-institute.org /pdf/cr_22.pdf.

30. A. A. Braga and B. J. Bond, "Policing crime and disorder hot spots: a randomized controlled trial," *Criminology*, vol. 46, no. 3, pp. 577–607, 2008.

31. United States Department of Justice, Federal Bureau of Investigation, "Crime in the United States," 2011, http://www.fbi.gov /about-us/cjis/ucr/crime-in-the-u.s/2010/crime-in-the-u.s.2010 /caution-against-ranking.

"DIVERSITY IN THE BRITISH POLICE: ADAPTING TO A MULTICULTURAL SOCIETY" BY BELA BHUGOWANDEEN

1. <http://www.cre.gov.uk/legal/rra/.html>

2. Notably Stuart Hall, Chas Critcher, Tony Jefferson, John Clark, Brian Roberts, *Policing the Crisis: Mugging, the State, and Law and Order*, London, Macmillan, 1978; Paul Gilroy, *There Ain't No Black in The Union Jack : The Cultural Politics of Race and Nation*, Hutchinson, 1987; Michael Keith, *Race, Riots and Policing: Lore and disorder in a multi-racist society*, London, UCL Press, 1993.

3. Bowling B., Phillips, C., 'Policing ethnic minority communities' originally published in Newburn, Tim, (ed.) *Handbook of policing*. Willan Publishing, Devon, UK, 2003 pp. 528-555, LSE Research online, July 2010, <http://eprints.lse.ac.uk/9576/1/Policing_ethnic_minority_communities_%28LSERO%29.pdf>, accessed 25 July 2013.

4. <http://www.cre.gov.uk/legal/rra/.html>

5. G., Berman, 'Police service strength' Standard Note: SN00634, House of Commons Library, 4 March 2013, p.3.

6. Marian Fitzgerald, Rae Sibbitt, "Ethnic monitoring in police

forces: A beginning", A Research and Statistics Directorate Report (London: Home Office) Home Office Research Study 173, 1997.

7. The CRE was replaced by the Commission for Equality and Human Rights (CEHR) in 2007.

8. <http://www.homeoffice.gov.uk>. The Police Human Resources Unit inside the Home Office is responsible for overseeing police numbers and recruitment

9. Lord Scarman, OBE, *The Scarman Report, The Brixton Disorders 10-12 April 1981*, London, Her Majesty's Stationery Office, 1986, p.126.

10. Ibid., p.132.

11. *The Stephen Lawrence Inquiry. Report of an Inquiry by Sir Willian MacPherson of Cluny*. February 1999; Michael Rowe, *Policing, Race and Racism*, Devon, Willan Publishing, 2004, p.61.

12. <http://www.statistics.gov.uk>.

13. Slough Race Equality Council, *Slough Demographics, An Analysis*, n.d. based on 2001 Census results.

14. <http://www.thamesvalley.police.uk/news_info.diversity/index.html>.

15. *Ibid.*

16. *Ibid.*

17. Foster, Newburn, Souhami, *Assessing the Impact of the Stephen Lawrence Inquiry*, London, Development and Statistics Directorate (Home Office Research Study 294) 2005, p.51.

18. *Ibid.*

19. *Ibid.*, p.61.

20. The headscarf worn by Muslim women.

21. The Race Relations Act 1976, www.statutelaw.gov.uk.

22. Thames Valley Black Police Association, online view, black in blue, <http://onlineview/bpa/about.htm>.

23. Michael Rowe, *Policing, Race and Racism*, Devon, Willan Publishing, 2004, p.20.

24. Alan Marlow, Barry Loveday, *After Macpherson, Policing after the Stephen Lawrence Inquiry*, Dorset, Russell House Publishing Ltd, 2000, p.111.

25. BBC News Online, 'Force admits rejecting white men', www.bbc.co.uk/news, 22 September 2006.

26. UK Statute Law Database, Ministry of Justice, Race Relations Act, Part IV, Clause 35, www.statutelaw.gov.uk.

27. Under section 37 of the Race Relations Act 1976. <http://www.cre.gov.uk/legal/rra.html>.

28. Simon Holdaway, *The Racialisation of British Policing*, London, Macmillan Press Ltd, 1996, p.144.

29. BBC Online, 'Police Plan to boost ethnic ranks', www.bbc .co.uk/news, 17 April 2004.
30. Statistics for the number and percentage of White and Ethnic Minority officers within the Thames Valley Police divided into different ranks in 2007.
31. *Home Office Citizenship survey in England and Wales*, 2003, K. Jansson, *Black and Minority Ethnic Groups' Experiences and Perceptions of Crime, Racially Motivated Crime and the Police: Findings from the 2004/5 British Crime Survey*, Home Office Online Report, 25/06, London, Home Office, 2006, quoted by Bowling, Parmar, Phillips, op.cit., p. 13.

CHAPTER 2: WHAT THE GOVERNMENT AND POLITICIANS SAY

"IMPROVING MOTIVATION AND PRODUCTIVITY OF POLICE OFFICERS" BY JAY FORTENBERY

[1] Kevin Gilmartin, *Emotional Survival for Law Enforcement: A Guide for Officers and Their Families* (Tucson, AZ: E-S Press, 2002).
[2] Stan Stojkovic, David Kalinich, and John Klofas, *Criminal Justice Organizations: Administration and Management* (Belmont, CA: Wadsworth, 2012).
[3] Micael Bjork, "Fighting Cynicism: Some Reflections on Self-Motivation in Police Work," *Police Quarterly* 11, no. 1 (March 2008): 88-101.
[4] Abraham Maslow, *Motivation and Personality* (New York, NY: Harper and Row, 1954).
[5] Stojkovic, Kalinich, and Klofas, *Criminal Justice Organizations.*
[6] Tracey Gove, "Praise and Recognition: The Importance of Social Support in Law Enforcement," *FBI Law Enforcement Bulletin*, October 2005, 14-19, *http://leb.fbi.gov/2005-pdfs/ leb-october-2005* (accessed January 26, 2015).
[7] Peter Finn, "Reducing Stress: An Organization-Centered Approach," *FBI Law Enforcement Bulletin*, August 1997, 20-26.
[8] Ibid.
[9] Ibid.
[10] Gove, "Praise and Recognition."
[11] Frederick Herzberg, Bernard Mausner, and Barbara Snyderman, *The Motivation to Work*, 2nd ed. (New York, NY: John

Wiley and Sons, 1959); and P.J. Ortmeier and Edwin Meese III, *Leadership, Ethics, and Policing: Challenges for the 21st Century,* 2nd ed. (Upper Saddle River, NJ: Prentice Hall, 2009).

[12] Bjork, "Fighting Cynicism."

[13] Ibid.

[14] Ibid.

[15] Robin Dreeke, "Self-Motivation and Self-Improvement," *FBI Law Enforcement Bulletin,* August 2008, under "Leadership Spotlight," *http://leb.fbi.gov/2008-pdfs/leb-august-2008* (accessed January 26, 2015).

[16] Ibid.

[17] Richard Johnson, "Officer Attitudes and Management Influences on Police Work Productivity," *American Journal of Criminal Justice* 36, no. 4 (December 2011): 293-306, *http://link .springer.com/ article/10.1007%2Fs12103-010-9090-2#* (accessed January 26, 2015).

[18] Kathy Harte, Kathleen Mahieu, David Mallett, Julie Norville, and Sander VanderWerf, "Improving Workplace Productivity: It Isn't Just About Reducing Absence," *Benefits Quarterly* (Third Quarter 2011): 13-26, *http://www.aon.com/attachments/ human-capital-consulting/Absence_Improving_ Workforce_ Productivity_5-7-13.pdf* (accessed January 26, 2015).

[19] Ibid.

[20] Daniel Shell, "Physical Fitness Tips for the Law Enforcement Executive," *FBI Law Enforcement Bulletin,* May 2005, 27-31, *http:// leb.fbi.gov/2005-pdfs/leb-may-2005* (accessed January 27, 2015).

[21] Ortmeier and Meese III, *Leadership, Ethics, and Policing.*

[22] Nathan Iannone, Marvin Iannone, and Jeffrey Bernstein, *Supervision of Police Personnel,* 7th ed. (Upper Saddle River, NJ: Pearson Prentice Hall, 2008).

[23] Ortmeier and Meese III, *Leadership, Ethics, and Policing.*

[24] Harry More and Larry Miller, *Effective Police Supervision,* 5th ed. (Cincinatti, OH: Anderson Publishing, 2007).

[25] Stojkovic, Kalinich, and Klofas, *Criminal Justice Organizations.*

[26] Kenneth Peak, *Justice Administration, Police, Courts, and Corrections Management,* 3rd ed. (Upper Saddle River, NJ: Prentice Hall, 2001).

[27] Robert Katz, "Skills of an Effective Administrator," *Harvard Business Review,* September 1974, *https://hbr.org/1974/09 /skills-of-an-effective-administrator/ar/1* (accessed January 27, 2015).

[28] Harte, Mahieu, Mallett, Norville, and VanderWerf, "Improving Workplace Productivity."

[29] Shell, "Physical Fitness Tips for the Law Enforcement Executive."

[30] Wayne Schmidt, "Weight and Fitness Requirements," *AELE*

Monthly Law Journal (December 2008): 201-208, *http://www.aele.org/
law/2008ALL12/2008-12MLJ201.pdf* (accessed January 27, 2015).

[31] Ronald Loeppke, Michael Taitel, Dennis Richling, Thomas
Parry, Ronald Kessler, Pam Hymel, and Doris Konicki, "Health
and Productivity as a Business Strategy: A Multiemployer
Study," *Journal of Occupational and Environmental Medicine* 49,
no. 7 (July 2007): 712-721, *http://www.acoem.org/ uploadedFiles
/Healthy_Workplaces_Now/HPM%20As%20a%20Business%20
Strategy.pdf* (accessed January 27, 2015).

[32] Ibid.

[33] Thomas Collingwood, Robert Hoffman, and Jay Smith, "Underlying Physical Fitness Factors for Performing Police Officer Physical Tasks," *The Police Chief* 71, no. 3 (March 2004), *http://www
.policechiefmagazine.org/magazine/index.cfm?fuseaction=display
_arch&article_id=251&issue_id=32004* (accessed January 27, 2015).

[34] Michael Caldero and John Crank, *Police Ethics: The Corruption of the Noble Cause*, rev. 3rd ed. (Burlington, MA: Anderson
Publishing, 2011).

[35] Finn, "Reducing Stress."

[36] Johnson, "Officer Attitudes and Management Influences on
Police Work Productivity."

[37] Shell, "Physical Fitness Tips for the Law Enforcement Executive."

[38] Harte, Mahieu, Mallett, Norville, and VanderWerf, "Improving
Workplace Productivity"; and Finn, "Reducing Stress."

CHAPTER 4: WHAT ADVOCACY
ORGANIZATIONS SAY

"STANDING BY POLICE VIOLENCE: ON THE
CONSTITUTION OF THE IDEAL CITIZEN AS
SOUSVEILLER" BY BEN BRUCATO

Ariel, Barak, William A. Farrar, and Alex Sutherland. "The Effect
of Police Body-Worn Cameras on Use of Force and Citizens'
Complaints against the Police: A Randomized Controlled Trial."
Journal of Quantitative Criminology 31.3 (2015): 509–35. Print.

Bauman, Zygmunt. "From Bystander to Actor." *Journal of Human
Rights* 2.2 (2003): 137–151. Print.

Benjamin, Walter. "On Some Motifs in Baudelaire." *Illuminations*.
New York: Schocken Books, 1969. 155–200. Print.

Boltanski, Luc. *Distant Suffering: Morality, Media, and Politics*.
Cambridge University Press, 1999. Print.

Borja, Mary E. Christopher Sharp v. Baltimore City Police Department, et. al. [letter], 14 May 2012. *USDOJ*. PDF. 7 July 2015.

Brighenti, Andrea Mubi. *Visibility in Social Theory and Social Research*. New York: Palgrave Macmillan, 2010. Print.

Brucato, Ben. "The Crisis and a Way Forward: What We Can Learn from Occupy Wall Street." *Humanity & Society* 36.1 (2012): 76–84. Print.

Brucato, Ben. "Fabricating the Color Line in a White Democracy: From Slave Catchers to Petty Sovereigns." *Theoria* 61.141 (2014): 30–54. Print.

Brucato, Ben. "Policing Made Visible: Mobile Technologies and the Importance of Point of View." *Surveillance & Society* 13.3–4 (2015): 455–73. *Surveillance-and-society.org*. PDF. 10 Oct. 2016.

Brucato, Ben. "The New Transparency: Police Violence in the Context of Ubiquitous Surveillance." *Media and Communication* 3.3 (2015): 39–55. Print.

Bruno, Fernanda. "A Brief Cartography of Smart Cameras: Proactive Surveillance and Control." *ICTs for Mobile and Ubiquitous Urban Infrastructures: Surveillance, Locative Media and Global Networks: Surveillance, Locative Media and Global Networks*. Hershey, PA: IGI Global, 2010. 257–71. Print.

Capehart, Jonathan. "Feidin Santana, Hero of North Charleston." *The Washington Post* 9 Apr. 2015. Web. 14 Aug. 2015.

Cheliotis, Leonidas K. "The Ambivalent Consequences of Visibility: Crime and Prisons in the Mass Media." *Crime, Media, Culture* 6.2 (2010): 169–84. Print.

Cohen, Stanley. *States of denial: Knowing about atrocities and suffering*. New York: John Wiley & Sons, 2013. Print.

Crary, Jonathan. *Techniques of the Observer: On Vision and Modernity in the Nineteenth century*. Cambridge, MA: MIT Press, 1992. Print.

Cushing, Tim. "Philly Transit Police Chief Shocked that No One Came to the Assistance of a Cop Being Assaulted by a Suspect." *TechDirt* 2 Oct. 2013. Web. 4 Sept. 2016.

Darley, John M., and Bibb Latane. "Bystander Intervention in Emergencies: Diffusion of Responsibility." *Journal of Personality and Social Psychology* 8.4 (1968): 377–83.

Farberov, Snejana. "Cops AArrest Man Who Sexually Assaulted a Sleeping Woman on New York Subway Train After Another Passenger Recorded Attack and Put it on YouTube Instead of Intervening." *Mail Online* 23 Mar. 2015. Web. 28 Mar. 2016.

Fernandez, Luis. *Policing Dissent: Social Control and the Anti-Globalization Movement*. New Brunswick, NJ: Rutgers UP, 2008. Print.

Feuer, Jane. "The Concept of Live Television: Ontology as Ideology." *Regarding Television* (1983): 12–22. Print.

Filipovic, Jill. "Two Years Ago, a Woman Was Sexually Assaulted

While Sleeping on the Subway and a Video Went Viral. Now
  She's Speaking Out." *Cosmopolitan* 24 Dec. 2014. *Cosmopolitan.
  com*. Web. 11 Oct. 2016.

Foucault, Michel. *Discipline and Punish: The Birth of the Prison*. New
  York: Random House, 1975. Print.

Goldsmith, Andrew John. "Policing's New Visibility." *The British
  Journal of Criminology* (2010): 914–34. Print.

Green, Jeffrey Edward. *The Eyes of the People: Democracy in an Age
  of Spectatorship*. New York: Oxford UP, 2010. Print.

Haggerty, Kevin D., and Richard V. Ericson. "The Surveillant Assem-
  blage." *The British Journal of Sociology* 51.4 (2000): 605–22. Print.

Kapuscinski, Ryszard. "Les médias reflètent-ils la réalité du
  monde?" *Manière de voir* 5 (2002): 50–55. Concours.agriculture.
  gouv.fr. PDF. 11 Oct. 2016.

Kearon, Tony. "Surveillance Technologies and the Crises of Confidence in Regulatory Agencies." *Criminology and Criminal Justice*
  (2012): 1–17. Print.

Kindy, Kimberly, and Kelly, Kimbriell. "Thousands Dead, Few
  Prosecuted." *The Washington Post* 11 Apr. 2015. *Washingtonpost.
  com*. Web. 11 Oct. 2016.

Leon, Harmon. "Cop Punches Occupy Wall Street Protester: The
  Whole World Is Watching!" *SF Gate* 10 Oct. 2011. Web. 3 Mar. 2014

Lyon, David. *Surveillance Society: Monitoring Everyday Life*. Milton
  Keynes: The Open UP, 2001. Print.

Lyon, David. "The Search for Surveillance Theories." *Theorizing
  Surveillance: The Panopticon and Beyond*. London: Willan Publishing (2006). 3–20. Print.

Mann, Steve, Jason Nolan, and Barry Wellman. "Sousveillance:
  Inventing and Using Wearable Computing Devices for Data
  Collection in Surveillance Environments." *Surveillance & Soci-
  ety* 1.3 (2002): 331–55. *Ojs.library.queens.ca*. PDF. 10 Oct. 2016.

Manning, Rachel, Mark Levine, and Alan Collins. "The Kitty
  Genovese Murder and the Social Psychology of Helping: The
  Parable of the 38 Witnesses." *American Psychologist* 62.6 (2007):
  555–62. Print.

Marx, Garty T. "Soft Surveillance: The Growth of Mandatory
  Volunteerism in Collecting Personal Information — 'Hey buddy
  can you spare a DNA?'" Torin Monahan, ed. *Surveillance and
  Security: Technological Politics and Power in Everyday Life*. London: Routledge, 2006. 37–56. Print.

Mathiesen, Thomas. "The Viewer Society: Michel Foucault's 'Panopticon' Revisited." *Theoretical Criminology* 1.2 (1997): 215–34. Print.

Milgram, Stanley, and Paul Hollander. "The Murder They Heard."
  The Nation 15 June 1964: 602–04. Print.

Miller, Carlos. "Ten Rules for Recording Cops and other Authority Figures." *Photography Is Not A Crime* 20 June 2014. *Photographyisnotacrime.com*. Web. 3 Aug. 2015.

Mitchell, W. J. T. "Realism and the Digital image." *Critical Realism in Contemporary Art: Around Allan Sekula's Photography*. Cornell UP, 2007. 12–27. Print.

Newell, Bryce Clayton. "Crossing Lenses: Policing's New Visibility and the Role of 'Smartphone Journalism' as a Form of Freedom-Preserving Reciprocal Surveillance." *Journal of Law, Technology, and Policy* 1 (2014): 59–104.

"NYPD white shirt KO's a protester at today's march 10/14/11." *YouTube* 14 Oct. 2011. Web. 3 Aug. 2015.

Oliver, Kelly. *Witnessing: Beyond Recognition*. Minneapolis: U of Minnesota P, 2001. Print.

Poe, Edgar Allan "The Man of the Crowd." *Edgar Allan Poe: Complete Tales & Poems*. 1840. Edison: NJ: Castle Books, 2002. 425–30. Print.

Robbins, Christopher. "HIV Positive Protester Says Cop Who Punched Him Should Get Tested." *Gothamist* 14 Oct. 2011. Web. Web. 18, 2015.

Sedgwick, Eve Kosofsky. *Touching Feeling: Affect, Pedagogy, Performativity*. Durham, NC: Duke UP, 2003. Print.

Sekula, Allan. "Dismantling Modernism, Reinventing Documentary: Notes on the Politics of Representation." *The Massachusetts Review* 19.4 (1978): 859–83. Print.

Simmel, Georg. "The Metropolis and Mental Life." *Georg Simmel: On Individuality and Social Forms*. 1903. Chicago: U of Chicago P, 1972. 324–39. Print.

Sontag, Susan. *Regarding the Pain of Others*. New York: Farrar, Straus & Giroux, 2003. Print.

Thompson, John B. "The New Visibility." *Theory, Culture & Society* 22.6 (2005): 31–51. Print.

White, Michael. *Police Officer Body-Worn Cameras: Assessing the Evidence*. Washington, DC: U.S. Department of Justice, Office of Community Oriented Policing Services, 2014. Print.

Williams, Kristian. "On the Potential Significance of Copwatching" [weblog comment]. *Unity & Struggle* 10 Nov. 2009. *Unityandstruggle.org*. Web. 18 Aug. 2015.

Yesil, Bilge. "Recording and Reporting: Camera Phones, User-Generated Images and Surveillance." Rodrigo J. Firmino, Fabio Duarte, and Covis Ultramari, eds. ICTs for Mobile and Ubiquitous Urban Infrastructures: Surveillance, Locative Media, and Global Networks. Hershey, PA: IGI Global, 2010. 272–93.

GLOSSARY

bias A tendency to view information in a way that leans toward one's already-held beliefs.

codicil An additional or supplemental piece of information made to clarify an existing text.

community policing A process by which police officers are assigned to neighborhoods to better interact with the population they serve by forming relationships with community members.

COMPSTAT An abbreviation of COMPuter STATistics, tools used by police departments modeled after the accountability processes of the New York City Police Department.

ethnic minority A group that has a different race, culture, or nationality than the largest population in an area.

excessive force The use of police action that is considered to be more than a situation warrants. Note: There is no legal definition or limit that clearly explains what excessive force is, and it is usually decided on a case-by-case basis.

hot spots Areas in a city, town, or neighborhood where criminal activity seems to be concentrated.

intersectionality A theory created by Kimberlé Williams Crenshaw to describe how multiple facets of a person, such as race, ethnicity, class, belief system, sexuality, gender, and disability, interact to create an identity that is unique from an identity seen through only one viewpoint.

justified force The use of police action that is considered to be appropriate for the situation. Note: There is no legal definition or limit that clearly explains what justified force is, and it is usually decided on a case-by-case basis.

misconduct Unacceptable or inappropriate behavior.

perpetrators Someone who carries out any kind of criminal activity.

racial profiling Basing one's suspicion of someone (for example, in committing an offense or a crime) on their race.

systemic Something that effects a whole system and not just individuals.

transactional leadership A leadership style in which those at the top of a hierarchy make all the decisions and do not empower those in lower levels to make any—or very few— decisions on their own.

transformational leadership A leadership style that empowers those at the lower levels of a hierarchy with the intent of bringing change and developing their skills to become higher-level leaders.

FOR MORE INFORMATION

Balko, Radley. *The Rise of the Warrior Cop: The Militarization of America's Police Forces*. New York, NY: PublicAffairs, 2013.

Coates, Ta-Nehisi. *Between the World and Me*. New York, NY: Spiegel & Grau, 2015.

Hill, Marc Lamont and Todd Brewster. *Nobody: Casualties of America's War on the Vulnerable, from Ferguson to Flint and Beyond*. New York, NY: Atria Books, 2016.

Jackson, Tiffany D. *Allegedly*. New York, NY: Katherine Tegen Books, 2017.

Miller, Linda S, Kären M. Hess, and Christine M.H. Orethmann. *Community Policing: Partnerships for Problem Solving: 6th Edition*. Boston, MA: Cengage Learning, 2010.

Nelson, Jill, ed. *Police Brutality, An Anthology*. New York, NY: W.W. Norton & Company, 2001.

Peak, Ken. *Justice Administration: Police, Courts, and Corrections Management*. New York, NY: Pearson, 2015.

Plantinga, Adam. *400 Things Cops Know: Street-Smart Lessons from a Veteran Patrolman*. Fresno, CA: Quill Driver, 2014.

Thomas, Angie. *The Hate U Give*. New York, NY: Balzer + Bray, 2017.

WEBSITES

Black Lives Matter (BLM)
blacklivesmatter.com
Black Lives Matter is the central website for the chapter-based organization with information on the movement, local chapter locator, and links to recent news.

Blue Lives Matter
bluelivesmatter.blue
Blue Lives Matter reports news from the perspective of law enforcement, and provides resources for them and their families.

Campaign Zero
joincampaignzero.org
Campaign Zero is the central website for the Campaign Zero project, a side effort that sprang from the Black Lives Matter movement. It provides data points and police recommendations on policing.

We the Protestors
wetheprotesters.org
We the Protesters is a central repository for information relating to activism regarding police activism in the US, including links to data, research, violence mapping, and other projects.

INDEX

A

Albuquerque, NM, police, 9
Amendments
  Eighth, 116, 127–128
  Fifth, 160
  First, 100–103, 160
  Fourteenth, 112, 114,
    116–118, 127–129
  Fourth, 9, 100–101,
    112–113, 114,
    132–134, 160

B

Baltimore, MD, 8, 195,
  203–206
Black and Minority Ethnic
  Recruitment Team, 57
Black Lives Matter, 4, 76,
  106–110, 181
Black Police Association,
  57–58, 65–68
Blue Lives Matter, 4
body cameras, 4, 19–21, 160
Bradford, Fred, 180
Bratton, William, 32–34
British police diversity,
  52–75
Brown, Michael, 4, 8, 139,
  155, 168, 179
Burgess, Bryan, 180
bystanders, 112–113, 150,
  152, 161–163, 166-167,
  170–175

C

California Highway Patrol,
  38, 138, 186
Canfield Watchmen,
  168–170
Cardona, Johnny, 152, 177
Cato Institute's National
  Police Misconduct
  Reporting Project,
  163–164
Centers for Disease Control
  and Prevention (CDC),
  14, 137, 138, 139–140
Chuva, Carlos, 173–174

civil rights, 77–79, 82, 86,
  186
Cleveland, OH, police, 8, 9
Comey, James B., 11–12,
  16–17
Commission for Racial
  Equality, 53
*Commonwealth v. Jimmy
  Warren*, 99, 107–110
community policing, 10,
  28–35, 39, 54–75, 80, 82,
  182, 187–194
COMPSTAT, 26–27, 33–34,
  36, 39, 42, 44, 46
constitutional rights, 85,
  102, 104, 105, 111, 123,
  128, 210
copwatching, 151, 166–170,
  186–187
crime control model, 26–27,
  33, 36, 37, 39, 40–46
crime data, 35, 40, 42, 46
Crutcher, Terence, 106

D

deadly police force, 9,
  12–13, 14, 16, 83, 100,
  111–113, 190
demographics, 11–12, 18,
  31, 45
directed crime prevention,
  32, 37–38
discrimination, 9, 16, 52,
  54, 58–59, 63, 69, 78, 106
DNA sampling and data-
  bases, 132–136
Duenez, Ernesto, Jr., 155

E

excessive police force,
  8–21, 83, 100, 111–113,
  114, 117–131, 168, 180

F

faulty frisk, 183–185
Federal Bureau of Investigation (FBI), 10, 11–12,
  14, 16–17, 45, 76, 135,
  190

Ferguson, MO, police,
  9–10, 11, 111, 139,
  155–156, 168, 179, 207,
  209–210
*Fields v. City of Philadel-
  phia and Geraci v. City
  of Philadelphia*, 99,
  100–105

G

Garner, Eric, 8, 156, 171
genetic information and
  privacy, 132–136
Genovese, Kitty, 170–172
Grant, Oscar, 155, 165–166,
  186
Gray, Freddie, 8–9, 195,
  203–206
Gray, Kimani, 179, 186

H

Hays, Ernest, 173
Hendrickson, Stan, 118
hot-spot policing, 6–7,
  22–25, 27, 35, 37, 40,
  46, 110
Human Rights Watch,
  143–144, 147

I

"If You See Something,
  Film Something" cam-
  paign, 163–165
immunity, 112, 127, 147–148
internet and social media,
  4, 21, 152–155, 164

K

Keunang, Charly "Africa"
  Leundeu, 157
King, Alonzo, 133, 134
King, Rodney, 4, 17,
  170–171, 178
Kingsley, Michael, 114,
  117–125, 130–131
Kingsley v. Hendrickson,
  100, 114–131

L

law enforcement ethics,
  47–51

Lawrence, Stephen, 52, 53
Lawson, Wayne, 207–211
less-lethal weapons, 18–19
Lopez, Elisa, 173–174
Los Angeles Police Department (LAPD), 156, 170

M
Macpherson Report, 52, 55, 56, 58, 68, 70
Maryland v. King, 100, 132–136
Massachusetts Supreme Judicial Court, 106–107, 108–110
media coverage, 21, 155, 179, 182, 195
Mendez, Joseph, 183–185
minority groups
confidence in law enforcement, 9–10
police recruits from, 52–53, 56–68, 68–75
relationship with law enforcement, 28, 54–55
targeting of, 52
Monroe, Susan, 187–194
Moody, John, 155

N
National Black Police Association, 57–58, 65
National Police Monitoring and Reporting Project, 150
New York Police Department (NYPD), 34, 36–37, 42, 152, 177, 179
Nestel, Thomas, 173
New Jim Crow, 186–187

O
Occupy movement, 151, 153, 154, 155, 178
Occupy Wall Street, 150–155, 162, 172, 177, 178
Operation Comfort, 63–65, 67

P
Pantaleo, Daniel, 156
Papua New Guinea
domestic violence in, 141–142, 146
relationship between police and women, 141–144, 146
reports of rape by police, 143–144
Perris Station, 26–27, 38–41, 42–45
Photography Is Not a Crime!, 166–168, 169
Pinnock, Marlene, 138–140, 185–187
Plumhoff v. Rickard, 100, 111–113
Police and Community Working Together (PACT) program, 188–194
police brutality, 78, 87, 166, 182, 185–187
against non-whites, 8–9, 14–18, 106, 107, 109–110, 139–140, 186–187, 196, 204
protests against, 4, 8, 106, 150, 168, 195, 202, 204–205, 208–210
police culture, 9, 50–51, 61, 79, 149
police misconduct, 10, 78–80, 84–87, 103, 159, 163, 165
police officers
assault of, 10, 90, 104, 173
health and fitness, 93, 95–97
"know your rights" training, 168
lack of training, 9, 144, 145, 148
motivation of, 88–98
physical training, 95, 97
productivity, 88–98
race relations training, 54–55, 58–60, 71, 80, 82–83
self-motivation, 91–92, 97
stress, 10, 78, 90, 91, 93, 97
training on use of force, 13, 15, 78, 80
transparency, 10, 20, 100–105, 169
Polish communities, 61, 74–75
positive discrimination, 69–74, 78
professional model of policing, 28, 32, 38, 46

R
Race Relations Acts, 52, 53, 56, 58, 69, 71
race relations training, 54–55, 58–60, 71, 80, 82–83
racial profiling, 16, 79, 80–81, 82–83, 86, 107, 109–110
racism, 21, 31, 55, 59, 62, 65, 75, 110, 197, 198–199, 201–202
rational-legal bureaucratic model of policing, 28
reasonable police force, 8, 12, 83, 115, 123, 126
recording police activity, 19, 100–105, 138, 150, 155–156, 160–166, 169, 170–174, 179, 180
reverse discrimination, 71–73
Rice, Tamir, 8

Rickard, Donald, 111, 113
riots, 8, 11, 54, 195,
    203–206, 207, 208, 210
Rivera-Pitre, Felix,
    151–152, 177–180
Riverside County Sheriff's
    Department, 26, 38,
    42–43
role models, 47, 73–74

S
Safe Outside the System
    Project, 186
Scarman Report, 55
Scott, Keith Lamont, 106
Scott, Walter, 8, 20, 156,
    171
Scott v. Harris, 12, 112
September 11, 2001, terror
    attacks, 62–63, 154
Slager, Michael T., 8, 156,
    171
Smiley, Jasheem, 174
sousveillance, 138, 158–
    161, 166, 170, 175
state of mind, 109, 114,
    120, 121–123, 130
statistics on use of force,
    11–12, 13–16
Stephen Lawrence
    Inquiry Report, 53, 55,
    58, 61, 66, 68
surveillance
    officer-worn cameras,
        4, 19–21, 160
    of police by citizens
        and bystanders,
        154–160, 161–163
    and sousveillance, 138,
        158–161, 166, 170,
        175
suspect characteristics,
    16–18

T
tasers, 18–19, 118, 122
Terry stops, 135, 136, 185
Terry v. Ohio, 135, 136

Thames Valley Black Police
    Association, 66–68
Thames Valley Police, 53,
    56–58, 60, 62, 69–70, 72,
    74–75
Thomas, Kelly, 155
three Rs of policing, 32
transactional leadership,
    47
transformational leader-
    ship, 47–51

U
unreasonable force, 94,
    114, 117, 119–120, 123,
    130, 131
US Commission on Civil
    Rights, 76–78
US Supreme Court, 12,
    99, 100, 102, 108, 111,
    114–131, 132–135

V
video documentation, 4,
    8, 138, 150–156, 164,
    166–180, 182, 187
    increased recordings,
        19–20
    legal right to record,
        100–105, 160
Violent Crime Control and
    Law Enforcement Act,
    85–86

W
Warren, Jimmy, 107–110
Washington, Samuel, 173
Wilson, Darren, 8, 155,
    168, 179

Z
Zuccotti Park, 151, 155

ABOUT THE EDITOR

Cyndy Aleo is a freelance writer and editor who changed her major to English from journalism when she realized she preferred editing. She is also parent to four children, three of them teens. This is her first book for Enslow Publishing.